VOCABULARY CONNECTIONS

Book II
Word Parts

VOCABULARY CONNECTIONS

Book II
Word Parts

Marianne C. Reynolds

Mercer County Community College

Boston, Massachusetts   Burr Ridge, Illinois   Dubuque, Iowa
Madison, Wisconsin   New York, New York   San Francisco, California   St. Louis, Missouri

McGraw-Hill Higher Education

*A Division of The **McGraw-Hill** Companies*

VOCABULARY CONNECTIONS: BOOK II WORD PARTS

10 11 12 13 14 15 16 DOC/DOC 0 9 8 7

ISBN: 978-0-07-052629-7
MHID: 0-07-052629-X

Vice president and editorial director: *Phil Butcher*
Sponsoring editor: *Sarah Moyers*
Marketing manager: *Lesley Denton*
Project manager: *Lynne Basler*
Production supervisor: *Karen Thigpen*
Senior designer: *Laurie J. Entringer*
Compositor: *Electronic Publishing Services, Inc. (TN)*
Typeface: *10/12 Palatino*
Printer: *R. R. Donnelley & Sons—Crawfordsville*

www.mhhe.com

*For Penny, Gary, Dave, Amy,
Laquane, and all my other students
who helped me develop and try
out the exercises in this book*

PREFACE

Many people would like to have a larger vocabulary. If you check the "self-help" section of a bookstore, you may find several books devoted to helping people learn new words. As with many other subjects, though, vocabulary is hard to learn on your own. Most of us benefit from the discipline and schedule a course provides that independent study does not. In addition to the advantage of studying vocabulary in a college course, you have the benefit of exposure to a variety of words in your other courses and academic activities. The business you are in as a college student is "word dependent." In your classes and your studies, you are constantly bombarded with words. You hear them; you see them; you write them. If you make a conscious effort to learn and remember the meanings of new words, you will find your "environment of words" a great help.

We can expand our vocabulary in several ways. As children, part of our normal development is language acquisition. For young children learning to speak, the rate of new words learned is phenomenal. They usually begin to use new words as labels for familiar people (*Mommy*) or objects (*cookie*). Adults who learn a new language also may begin by asking the names of objects: "What is this called?" or "How do you say *casa* [house] in English?" For both groups, this language learning is an exciting and rewarding process. Those of you who begin to work or study in a new field will also be exposed to a new vocabulary. A student who began a new job in a warehouse learned the term *palletizing*. Computer science students may learn a new meaning for the word *bursting*, as it applies to paper instead of balloons.

As a college student, your vocabulary development may not be as dramatic as that of a young child or a non-native speaker. But you will learn new words as you read and listen. Your professors may use words with which you are unfamiliar, and you may find new words in your textbooks and course-related reading. In many cases, these words will be the same, and the more often you meet them, the more likely you will learn and remember their meanings. A conscious effort on your part will make learning vocabulary easier. You may even enjoy it!

Learn to look for clues as you hear or read an unfamiliar word. In class, your professor may spontaneously provide a definition, or a student may ask for one. You may be able to tell the word's meaning from the context, the way it is used. The speaker's gestures, tone of voice, or the spelling of the word on the board may help as well. In print, you can use the context, a supplied definition, a glossary, or your dictionary as aids.

If you had the luxury of unlimited time to expand your vocabulary, you could probably rely solely on your exposure to new words, terms, and phrases. To be a successful college learner, though, you should probably make a more deliberate effort to learn most of the words you will meet in college situations. The English language is rich with synonyms, allowing readers and speakers to select words that clearly and specifically communicate their meanings. As a reader and listener, you will learn the meanings of many words that can be used interchangeably. Although it is admirable if you choose to incorporate many of the words you learn this semester into your speaking and writing vocabulary, your primary goal this semester should be recognition. When you complete the work in this textbook, you still may not be able to write from memory all the definitions you learned. If you learned them well, however, when you first studied them, you should be able to recall their meanings when you meet them in context in the future.

The texts in this series are designed to be practical. The three books can be used in any order. In fact, the order of the chapters within each book can be changed as well.

The first book deals with general vocabulary. Many college professors claim that they can teach their students the course-related terminology, but they also expect them to be knowledgeable about general, frequently used, college-level words. In this book, you will learn many words that can neither be defined by their word parts nor associated with a particular field. They are words that will come up in lectures, textbooks, newspaper and journal articles, and conversation among educated people. They were selected from high-frequency word lists, so you know you can count on seeing them again. Many instructors choose to begin with this book and teach the word parts and academic words later in the semester.

The second book concentrates on word parts—prefixes, suffixes, and roots. You will learn the meanings of the word parts and many words they make up. You may begin to think of words as puzzles. You can analyze words by identifying their parts to discover their meanings. You can also synthesize the word parts by putting them together to make new words. Learning word parts is a very efficient way to increase your vocabulary. There are so many English words that can be defined if you know the meanings of their parts. The benefits of your study time will be multiplied as you are able to unlock the meanings of a tremendous number of words. You will also find yourself using word parts of words you already know to help define new ones.

The third book presents words in academic context. College students take reading or first-year experience courses to help them do well in their college course work. The most practical way to teach you how to define unfamiliar words when you meet them in your textbooks is to give you some samples. The subject fields are representative of courses most college students take during their first or second year. Certainly you won't learn all the vocabulary you need for your psychology or biology course in a chapter. But you will learn some key terms in each field and practice using textbook material to define them. You may also be surprised at how many of these terms are defined in the text and how many others' meanings you can figure out.

In addition to working through the exercises in this book and studying for the quizzes and tests, you may want to keep a personal journal. Some students find it beneficial to keep a record of unfamiliar words they meet on a daily basis. A note indicating the word, where you encountered it, and a brief definition is all that is necessary. Many of my students report that they find themselves recording the same word several times until they learn it. This experience shows the need to study as well as to write down unfamiliar words. It also supports the notion that some words occur more frequently than others and recommends their mastery. Research has shown that recreational or "free" reading also increases vocabulary development. Many college students complain that they barely have time to complete their course-related reading. Nevertheless, those who devote 20 minutes a day to reading for pleasure (a newspaper, magazine, novel, or nonfiction book) report a gain in word knowledge as well as other benefits.

Study often. Brief daily study sessions are better than a long cramming session just before a test. Study with classmates, discuss the meanings of the words, and make them your own. Tell someone who is curious about words an interesting new term you have learned. Ask someone to quiz you on the word meanings. Try to use one new word a day in your conversation or writing. Pay attention to words and don't be afraid to try them out. You may be surprised at the number of people who are interested in the origins of words and their meanings.

Marianne C. Reynolds

CONTENTS

Book II

INTRODUCTION

There are 10 chapters in this book that introduce common word parts—prefixes, suffixes, and roots—word families, and dictionary instruction. Studying word parts is an efficient way to increase your vocabulary as there are many English words that can be defined if you know the meanings of the word parts that make them up. In most chapters, the word parts are grouped according to function (prefix, suffix, or root) or meaning. For example, word parts in one chapter all relate to time, and in another, all prefixes deal with numbers. There is no meaning theme for the chapters that present roots or suffixes. Rather, the most common roots and suffixes are included. Some of the chapters present groups of related words as word families. The chapters in this book can be arranged in any order. Some instructors prefer to begin with prefixes, and others choose to start with roots or word families. Many instructors begin with Chapter 10, the dictionary chapter; others save it until the end and use it as a departure point for students to work with actual dictionaries. In addition to the meanings of the word parts, each chapter has a word list, which includes the words presented in the chapter. The list gives the correct pronunciation, part of speech, and definition for each word.

A *prefix* is a word part that is found at the beginning of a word. It has a meaning of its own, and, when added to a word, can significantly change that word's meaning. For example, there is a big difference between the words *honest* and *dishonest.* The prefix *dis*, which means not, reverses the word's meaning. Usually the knowledge of prefix meanings alone will not allow you to figure out the total meaning of an unfamiliar word, but it is a big help. If you pay attention to prefixes as you read for pleasure or academic purposes, you will be able to understand the author's meaning more precisely.

A *root* is the heart, basis, or essence of a word. Knowing the meaning of the root is usually essential to figuring out the word's meaning. Words may consist of only roots, such as the word *equal,* or a root plus affixes (prefixes or suffixes). For example, in the word *intercept,* the root is *cep* (take or receive). The prefix *inter* (between) indicates that something has come between the object and the intended receiver. A football player may intercept a pass, or a spy may intercept a message intended for his enemy.

A *suffix* is a word part that comes at the end of a word. It often clarifies the type of word. For example, the suffixes *or* and *er* indicate that the word is naming a person. Another common suffix is *able* which means capable of. Some examples are words like *readable, agreeable,* and *understandable.*

You will also study from chapters that include word families, groups of words that share the same word parts and are related in meaning. An aid to vocabulary development is a knowledge of the relationships among words. The more word parts you learn, the more likely you will be to use them in deciphering unfamiliar words. As you begin to see the interrelationships among words, you will find more clues in the words whose meanings you are trying to unlock.

Each chapter contains five exercises that will allow you to practice using and defining the word parts. When you finish the chapter, your instructor will probably ask you to take a quiz. You may also be asked to take a cumulative test that covers two chapters.

Pronunciation Key

Use the following simple pronunciation guide to help you pronounce the words you will study. A sample word is provided for each vowel symbol that is used in the word lists.

	Short Vowels (indicated with no mark)		*Long Vowels* (indicated with a straight line called a macron above the letter)
a	hat	ā	say, hate
e	bet	ē	me, seat
i	tin	ī	fine, sky
o	pot	ō	so, rode
u	cut	ū	mule, use

The schwa (ə) is a very common sound in the English language. It has the sound of "uh" and can be made by any vowel. Examples follow:

a	in above	(ə buv′)
e	in system	(sis′ təm)
u	in circus	(sûr′ kəs)

The doubled oo takes on a short or long sound, too.

Short		*Long*	
oo	cook	o͞o	boot

Additional Vowel Sounds

ä	father	ô	order, raw
â	air	û	term, urge

WORD PARTS THAT INDICATE TIME   1

The word parts that are included in this chapter convey some meaning about time. Some are prefixes, and some are roots. In most cases, they appear at the beginning of words. For example, the prefix *re* (review or reread) and the root *arche* (archeology) usually start words. Other roots, like *chrono* may appear at the beginning (chronological) or in the middle (synchronize) of a word. When you find one of these word parts, it often adds information about *when,* or *how often,* or *in what kind of time order*. Consider, for example, the words *pre-test* and *post-test*. These prefixes tell you that the *pre-test* will happen before (instruction, placement, a course, etc.) and the *post-test* will happen after such activities.

A prefix is a word part that appears at the beginning of the word. Although it cannot stand on its own, it has its own meaning. A prefix adds to or changes the meaning of the word to which it is attached. When figuring out the meanings of new words, it is usually not sufficient to know only the meaning of the prefix. Knowledge of the meaning of the root is usually necessary as well.

A root forms the heart or essence of a word. It may be found in the middle, or at the beginning or end of a word, depending on whether prefixes and suffixes are attached.

In the list of word parts you will study in this chapter, the following are prefixes:

> ante   post   pre   re   semi

These prefixes need to be attached to a root to create a meaningful word.

The following word parts are usually considered roots, although they may appear at the beginning of a word:

> anni   arche   brevi   chrono   sequi

Each has a meaning that will form the essence of a word.

The following list contains 10 word parts that indicate something about time and examples of how they are used. A word list follows; then, practice exercises allow you to define words that contain these prefixes, combine word parts, and use words correctly.

Word Parts	Meaning	Examples
1. anni, annu, enni	year	anniversary, bicentennial
2. ante	before, in front of	antecedent, anteroom
3. arche	ancient	archaeology, archaic
4. brevi	brief	abbreviation, brevity
5. chrono	time	chronological, synchronize
6. post	after	postpone, postscript
7. pre	before	prefix, preview
8. re	again, do over	reread, remember
9. semi	half	semiweekly, semicircle
10. sequi	following	sequel, consequence

WORD LIST

The words in the following list include the word parts that you are studying in this chapter. Some of the words you have met as you reviewed the meanings of the word parts and sample words. Others you will learn as you complete the exercises and the quiz for this chapter. Most of the words you will need to answer the questions are found in this list. You can also rely on your own word knowledge and a dictionary, if you wish. Included in each word's listing is the pronunciation, part of speech, and definition. Dictionaries consulted in creating this text are listed in the Bibliography at the back of the book.

1. **abbreviation** (ə brē vē ā′ shən) *n:* shortened form of a word or phrase: *Mr. (Mister).*

2. **anniversary** (an ə vûr′ sər ē) *n:* **1.** the date on which an event occurred in a previous year. **2.** the celebration of the event: *a wedding anniversary party.*

3. **annual** (an′ yōō əl) *adj:* **1.** happening or recurring every year. **2.** yearly. *n:* **3.** a plant that lives for only one year. **4.** a publication issued once a year.

4. **antecedent** (an tə sē′ dent) *adj:* **1.** preceding; going or occurring before. *n:* **2.** a person or event that comes before or precedes. **3.** *Gram:* the word, phrase, or clause to which a relative pronoun refers: <u>John</u> *was disappointed when he was not elected president.*

5. **anteroom** (an′ tē rōōm) *n:* waiting room; lobby; entrance foyer.

6. **archaic** (ar kā′ ik) *adj:* **1.** belonging to an earlier time. **2.** no longer used or current; old-fashioned. **3.** *Lang.:* characterizing a word that was used at one time but is no longer in use.

7. **archeology** (ar kē ol′ ə jē) *n:* the study of early human life and cultures based on the recovery of remains and artifacts.

8. **chronic** (kron′ ik) *adj:* lasting a long time or recurring: *a chronic liar; a chronic backache.*

9. **chronological** (kron ə loj′ i kəl) *adj:* arranged in order of occurrence: *a chronological list of events.*

10. **consequence** (kon′ sə kwens) *n:* the result or outcome of something that happened before.

11. **postscript** (pōst′ skript) *n:* a sentence or brief message added to the end of an already completed letter. *Abbr.:* *P.S.* or *p.s.*

12. **postpone** (pōst pōne′) *v:* to delay or put off to some future time.

13. **predict** (prē dikt′) *v:* to tell in advance or before an event happens; to foretell; to prophesy; to make a prediction.

14. **preliminary** (prə lim′ ə ner ē) *adj:* before the main part or event; introductory.

15. **rearrange** (rē ə rānj′) *v:* to arrange or order again, esp. in a new way.

16. **reproduce** (rē prō dōōs) *v:* **1.** to make a copy. **2.** *Biol.:* to produce offspring. **3.** to produce again.

17. **semicircle** (sem′ i sûr′ kəl) *n:* half of a circle.

18. **semicolon** (sem′ i kō lən) *n:* a punctuation mark indicating a greater separation than a comma, but not as much as a period.

19. **sequel** (sē′ kwəl) *n:* **1.** something that follows or continues. **2.** a literary work that continues the narrative of an earlier work.

20. **synchronize** (sin′ krə nīz) *v:* **1.** to occur at the same time. **2.** to cause to indicate the same time, as wristwatches. **3.** to cause to operate at the same time or in unison.

Exercise 1: Complete the Word

In the sentences below, select one of the word parts to complete the underlined word. Then write a definition for the word you have formed.

a. annu   d. brevi   g. pre   i. semi
b. ante   e. chrono   h. re   j. sequ
c. arche   f. post

b 1. The English teacher conducted a lesson about identifying
_____*ante*cedents in sentences that came from the
students' essays.
before

j 2. Fans of the mystery writer Sue Grafton are always anxious
to read her latest _____*sequ*el in the Kinsey Milhone
investigations.
something that follows

i 3. Members of the soccer team formed a _____*semi*circle
with the captain in the middle to lead the warmup exercises.
half of a circle.

f 4. When her tooth stopped hurting, Iliana decided to
_____*post*pone her appointment with her dentist.
after

c 5. Fascinated by tools used by primitive people, Marisol hoped
to become an _____*arche*ologist one day.
The person who study early human life + culture

d 6. Gunther used so many personal ab_____*brevi*_____ations that
fellow-students could not decipher his notes.
Shortened form of a word or phrase

a 7. Townspeople looked forward to the _____*annu*al
Memorial Day parade and picnic as a time to visit with
their friends and neighbors.
happening or recurring every year.

g 8. During _____ *preliminary* hearings, residents and students commented on the school budget before it was put up for a vote.

before the main part or event.

e 9. The family photo albums were arranged in _____ *chrono* logical order beginning with the grandparents' wedding pictures.

arranged in order of occurrence

h 10. Whenever he read an article that related to his courses, Professor Gurgis _____ *re* produced it and distributed copies to his students.

to make a copy

Exercise 2: Select a Word

Use one of the words you have studied in this lesson to match the definition provided.

archeology 1. the study of ancient cultures.

sequel 2. a follow-up novel of a best-seller by the same author.

rearrange 3. to move pieces of furniture into different positions.

synchronize 4. to set two watches for exactly the same time.

consequences 5. something that happens as a result of a previous action.

abbreviation 6. a shortened form.

semicolon 7. a punctuation mark that indicates a significant pause.

preliminary 8. describing introductory remarks before a main speech.

postpone 9. to put something off to the future.

annual 10. the celebration of a wedding date.

Exercise 3: Use the Words in Context

In the following reading selection, you will find 10 numbered spaces. From the list of words that follows, select the word that fits best in each space.

As a graduate student in ____1____, Michael's advisor invited him to join a project related to some recent findings in Egypt. As a ____2____ activity to the field work, Michael's task was to organize the research that had been done already and label the artifacts in ____3____ order. He would then be able to construct a time-line illustrating the development of the civilization. Professor Mueller had decided to ____4____ a field trip to Egypt until his group of scholars and students had thoroughly learned what had already been discovered by other researchers. He ____5____ that this could be accomplished within a month if the information was organized. As a ____6____ of his new responsibilities, Michael chose to carry a lighter course load than usual, and devoted himself to the project for many hours each day. As Professor Mueller realized how overwhelming Michael's task was, he assigned two other students to help out. Since their working space was quite limited, the three had to ____7____ their schedules so that they didn't all show up at the same time. In addition, they had to be careful that their notes were meaningful to the others. Michael had to abandon his personal shorthand and write everything out instead of using ____8____. When the students had completed their work, Professor Mueller had the information ____9____ and distributed to all members of the department. At the ____10____ department dinner, the professor lavishly praised the work of the three students and announced that the field work would begin the next month.

_C_ 1.	a. abbreviations
_g_ 2.	b. annual
_d_ 3.	c. archeology
_h_ 4.	d. chronological
_f_ 5.	e. consequence
_e_ 6.	f. predicted

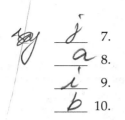

_d_ 7.

_a_ 8.

_i_ 9.

_b_ 10.

g. preliminary

h. postpone

i. reproduced

j. synchronize

Exercise 4: Use the Word Correctly

The sentences below contain underlined words that use the word parts you have studied. Indicate whether the words are used correctly (C) or incorrectly (I).

_I_ 1. Stan thought his parents' ideas about curfews for a seventeen-year-old were unreasonably <u>archaic</u>.

_I_ 2. After the championship basketball game, the sports editor <u>predicted</u> the victory and praised the high scorers.

_C_ 3. Unable to <u>postpone</u> taking her math test any longer, Dorothea arrived at the testing center at 5:30 on Friday.

_I_ 4. Testifying to Doctor Figueroa's popularity, his <u>anteroom</u> is always filled with patients.

_I_ 5. The chairman closed the meeting with some <u>preliminary</u> remarks and then called for a motion to adjourn.

_I_ 6. As a new speaker and writer of English, Lee's essays were difficult to read because he failed to use <u>semicolons</u> to indicate the end of his sentences.

_C_ 7. At the start of the swim meet, the two judges <u>synchronized</u> their stopwatches to insure agreement.

_C_ 8. Aimee's classmates considered her a <u>chronic</u> liar because of the one time she cheated on a test and then denied it.

_C_ 9. Although Max's use of <u>abbreviations</u> made his report shorter, it also made it more difficult to understand.

_C_ 10. The creative artist spent hours in his studio trying to <u>reproduce</u> the works of the great masters that he had studied as a youngster.

Exercise 5: Complete Analogies

Analogies are similarities between the characteristics or features of two things. They are the basis of a comparison. For example, a car uses fuel as its source of energy, as a human uses food as its source of energy.

The term *analogy* also infers a form of reasoning involving pairs of words that have particular relationships to each other. Readers are asked to complete analogies on the basis of their word knowledge and what they can deduce about the relationship between a pair of words. For example,

dog : puppy :: cat : kitten

is an analogy based on the relationship of adult to baby of the same species. An analogy is read: "dog is to puppy as cat is to kitten."

There are other types of analogy relationships. The words may be opposites, synonyms, part as to whole, category as to example, and others. Your task in the exercise that follows is to determine the relationship between the first pair of words, and then select a word that establishes the same type of relationship for the second pair. Here is a sample:

mathematics : algebra :: science : <u>Biology</u>

Acceptable answers include: biology, chemistry, physics, geology, and others. The relationship can be described as *category: example* or *whole: part*. Algebra is a branch or type of mathematics. It can be considered an example or a part. To complete the analogy, the final term should be a branch or type of science.

Select the best word to complete each analogy below.

a. archaic	c. postpone	e. semicircle
b. chronic	d. reproduction	f. synchronize

_____ *c*   1. judge : evaluate :: agree : *postpone*

_____   2. concert : videotape :: original : *reproduction*

_____   3. energetic : lazy :: modern : *archaic*

_____ *e*   4. whole : half :: circle : *semicircle*

_____   5. nervous : relaxed :: *synchronize* infrequent

g. abbreviation   i. chronological   k. predict
h. anniversary   j. consequence   l. preliminary

_j_ 6. provisions : supplies :: *consequences* : result
_l_ 7. introductory : main :: *preliminary* : keynote
_h_ 8. death : memorial :: wedding : *anniversary*
_k_ 9. invent : create :: *predict* : foretell
_i_ 10. daisy : flower :: *chronological* : order

PREFIXES THAT INDICATE POSITION OR DIRECTION   2

Many prefixes indicate position or direction. When you attach one of them to a root, you will provide additional information that often indicates "where." For example, the root *port* means carry. Different prefixes can tell you where something is being carried or sent, as in:

*im*port	carry or send into a country
*ex*port	carry or send out of the country
*trans*port	carry or send across the country.

The following list contains 10 prefixes that indicate position or direction and examples of how they are used. A word list follows; then, practice exercises allow you to define words that contain these prefixes, combine word parts, and use words correctly.

	Prefix	*Meaning*	*Examples*
1.	centri, centro	middle, center	central, egocentric
2.	circum	around	circumference, circumstance
3.	dia	through	diameter, diagnose
4.	en	into	entrance, engrave
5.	epi	upon	epidermis, epoxy
6.	im, in	into	immerse, inspect
7.	prim	first	primer, primary
8.	pro	forward, toward	propel, promote
9.	tele	distant	telephone, telecommunications
10.	trans	across	transport, transmit

<u>Notes</u>

1. The prefix *in* can also mean "not," as in the words *incorrect* or *incapable*. In this chapter, however, we will be considering *in* only in situations where it means "into."

2. There are two pronunciations for the word *primer*, depending on its meaning. When it refers to a book that is used to teach elementary school children to read, the pronunciation is (prim′ ər). When it is used to mean the first coat of paint, it is pronounced (prī′ mər).

WORD LIST

The words in the following list include the prefixes that you are studying in this chapter. Some of the words you have met as you reviewed the meanings of the prefixes and sample words. Others you will learn as you complete the exercises and the quiz for this chapter. To complete the exercises, you should rely on the words in this list, your own word knowledge, and a dictionary if you wish. Included in each word's listing is the pronunciation, part of speech, and definition.

1. **centralize** (sen′ trə līz) *v:* to bring to a central point or under one authority.

2. **circumference** (sûr kəm′ fər əns) *n:* the perimeter or boundary of a circle.

3. **circumvent** (sûr kəm vent′) *v:* **1.** to avoid, usually by strategy or cleverness. **2.** to go around. **3.** to defeat or entrap.

4. **diagnose** (dī′ əg nōs) *v:* **1.** to identify a disease by examination or tests. **2.** to determine the cause of something.

5. **diameter** (dī am′ ə tər) *n:* a straight line passing through the center of a circle.

6. **egocentric** (ē gō sen′ trik) *adj:* self-centered; having little regard for others.

7. **enclose** (en clōz′) *v:* **1.** to surround on all sides. **2.** to place in an envelope along with something else.

8. **engrave** (en grāv′) *v:* **1.** to carve, cut, or etch a design into a hard surface. **2.** to print from an engraved plate.

9. **epidermis** (ep ə dûr′ mis) *n:* the outer layer of skin.

10. **epoxy** (i pox′ ē) *n:* a synthetic resin used in adhesives and coatings.

11. **immerse** (i mûrs′) *v:* **1.** to plunge or dip into a liquid. **2.** to involve deeply: *immerse oneself in work.* **3.** to baptize by immersion.

12. **implant** (im′ plant) *v:* **1.** to establish firmly: *implant an idea in someone's mind.* **2.** to plant firmly in the ground. **3.** to insert into the body.

13. **primary** (prī′ mer ē) *adj:* **1.** first in order, time, rank, or importance. *n:* **2.** a preliminary election.

14. **primer** (prim′ ər) *n:* **1.** an introductory book, usu. for teaching children to read. (prī′ mər) **2.** one who primes. **3.** a device for igniting an explosive. **4.** an undercoat of paint.

15. **promote** (prə mōt′) *v:* **1.** to advance in rank. **2.** to encourage or help to grow. **3.** to advocate or work in behalf of. **4.** to try to make popular.

16. **propel** (prə pel′) *v:* to cause to move forward; to drive.

17. **telecommunication** (tel′ i kə myōō ni kā′ shən) *n:* the art and science of communicating over long distances as by radio, television, radar, telephone, computer.

18. **telescope** (tel′ ə skōp) *n:* a device used to make distant objects appear larger through the use of lenses.

19. **transmit** (trans mit′) *v:* **1.** to send on or transfer. **2.** to communicate, as information. **3.** to cause to spread, as a disease or infection.

20. **transport** (trans port′) *v:* **1.** to move, carry, or convey from one place to another. **2.** to carry away with emotion.

Exercise 1: Complete the Word

In the sentences below, select one of the word parts to complete the underlined word. Then write a definition for the word you have formed.

a. centr	d. en	g. prim	i. tele
b. circum	e. epi	h. ~~pro~~	j. trans
c. dia	f. im		

_____ 1. The author of the new diet cookbook appeared on several

morning TV talk shows to _____*pro*_____ mote her book sales.

_____

_____ 2. Doctor Fisher assured her patient that she would have a

_____ nosis as soon as the final test results arrived.

_____

_____ 3. After accepting a job in San Diego, Charles faced the task of

arranging to _____ port his belongings, family, pets,
and two cars from Pennsylvania.

_____

_____ 4. Matt felt his gender was a disadvantage when applying for teaching jobs in _____ary schools.

_____

_____ 5. The accident victim's burns fortunately were limited to the _____dermis.

_____

_____ 6. Fascinated by technology and advertising, Sofia decided to major in _____communications.

_____

_____ 7. An accused rapist was able to _____vent the law for seven years by fleeing the country and receiving financial support from his parents.

_____

_____ 8. After the governor cut the state college's budget by $8 million, the dean felt forced to _____alize several academic departments under a single head.

_____

_____ 9. Sue and John asked the jeweler to _____grave their initials and wedding date on the inside of their wedding rings.

_____

_____ 10. Although the label on her electric shaver indicated it was waterproof, Maxine thought she should not _____merse it in the tub.

_____

Exercise 2: Select a Word

Use one of the word parts you have studied in this lesson to create a word that matches the definition provided.

_____ 1. a synthetic material used as in gluing.

_____ 2. conceited.

_____ 3. to send from a distance.

_____ 4. a line that divides a circle in half.

_____ 5. a situation that would influence an event.

_____ 6. to establish.

_____ 7. to cause movement.

_____ 8. to include in a mailing.

_____ 9. a first coat of paint.

_____ 10. the distance around a circle.

Exercise 3: Use the Words in Context

In the following reading selection, you will find 10 numbered spaces. From the list of words that follows, select the word that fits best in each space.

After graduating with a business administration degree, Danielle considered herself fortunate to land a job with a large Boston investment firm. With the exception of her ____1____ boss who believed himself naturally superior to everyone, she enjoyed her colleagues as well as her work. When she had been with the organization for two years, rumors circulated that the company planned to ____2____ its operations, combining some departments, moving some people, and eliminating some positions. Although pleased when her boss told her she had been ____3____ to supervisor of trading, she had mixed feelings about the accompanying transfer to Atlanta. Danielle had always lived in Massachusetts, and she knew she would miss family, friends, and familiar surroundings. In addition, she wondered how she would ____4____ all her possessions and her cats. In her present ____5____, she had no need of a car. In Atlanta, however, she didn't know where she would live or what public transportation would be available. When she expressed her misgivings to her boss, he told her this opportunity was too good to pass up. He had recommended her, and he expected credit for selecting the ideal person for the job. Her ____6____ task would be to ____7____ the causes of the trading department's inefficiency. He expected her to move quickly, ____8____ herself in her work, and ____9____ her recommendations to increase the department's productivity by fax within a month. In a whirlwind two weeks, Danielle had packed, located an apartment in Atlanta, bought a car, received an ____10____ plaque from her colleagues in Boston, and driven south with her cats.

_____ 1.   a. transport

_____ 2.   b. transmit

_____ 3.   c. promoted

_____ 4.   d. primary

_____ 5.   e. immerse

_____ 6.   f. engraved

_____ 7.   g. diagnose

_____ 8.   h. circumstances

_____ 9.   i. egocentric

_____ 10.   j. centralize

Exercise 4: Use the Word Correctly

The sentences below contain underlined words that use the word parts you have studied. Indicate whether the words are used correctly (C) or incorrectly (I).

_____ 1. Since Jay would be out of town at election time, he planned to vote by epoxy.

_____ 2. The original engine did not have sufficient power to propel the boat through heavy seas.

_____ 3. Though the apologetic letter from the theater manager indicated that complimentary tickets were enclosed, Grace could not find them.

_____ 4. To monitor the territorial patterns of bears, the wildlife biologist implanted tracking devices under their skin.

_____ 5. Lucille measured the diameter of the circular garden by walking around the entire boundary.

_____ 6. The first-graders' faces glowed with excitement when Ms. Diaz passed out their primers and began their first reading lesson.

_____ 7. Martin circumvented the law by volunteering to help the police in their investigation.

_____ 8. The surgeon made a deep incision into the patient's abdomen, finally reaching the epidermis.

_____ 9. Donna's field work in <u>telecommunications</u> included a part-time position with the local radio station.

_____ 10. Members of the baseball team decided to buy fitted uniform hats, so the coach measured the <u>circumference</u> of each player's head.

Exercise 5: Complete Analogies

Select the best word to complete each analogy below.

a. circumference   c. diagnose   e. telescope
b. diameter   d. promote   f. transmit

_____ 1. transport : goods :: _____ : message

_____ 2. decline : advance :: demote : _____

_____ 3. microscope : bacteria :: _____ : stars

_____ 4. solve : problem :: _____ : illness

_____ 5. square : diagonal :: circle : _____

g. centralize   i. enclose   k. immerse
h. egocentric   j. engrave   l. primary

_____ 6. reproduce : copy :: carve : _____

_____ 7. delete : omit :: insert : _____

_____ 8. archaic : old :: _____ : beginning

_____ 9. integrate : segregate :: _____ : scatter

_____ 10. predict : foretell :: submerge : _____

PREFIXES THAT INDICATE SIZE OR NUMBER

3

Many prefixes carry numerical or size information. For example, you would easily know that the difference between a *bicycle* and a *tricycle* is one wheel, since the prefix *bi-* means two and the prefix *tri-* means three. As you learned in the first two chapters, knowing the meaning of these prefixes is not enough to reveal the meaning of the whole word. You also have to know or figure out the root's meaning as well. In the previous example, if you did not know the meaning of *cycle*, familiarity with the numerical prefixes alone would not allow you to define the words.

The following list contains 10 prefixes that indicate size or number and examples of how they are used. This is not an exhaustive list. You can probably think of other prefixes you know that also indicate size or number. A word list follows; then, practice exercises allow you to define words that contain these prefixes, combine word parts, and use words correctly.

	Prefix	*Meaning*	*Examples*
1.	bi	two, twice	bicycle, bilingual
2.	dec, deca	ten	decade, decimal
3.	demi	half, lesser	demigod, demitasse
4.	micro	small	microscope, microwave
5.	mini	small or reduced size	minibus, minimum
6.	mono	one, single	monopoly, monotonous
7.	multi	many, much	multiply, multicultural
8.	pent	five	pentagon, pentameter
9.	quad	four	quadrangle, quadruplet
10.	tri	three	triceratops, trio

WORD LIST

The words in the following list include the prefixes that you are studying in this chapter. Some of the words you have met as you reviewed the meanings of the prefixes and sample words. Others you will learn as you complete the exercises and the quiz for this chapter. Not all of the words you will need to answer the questions are found in this list. You will also need to rely on your own word knowledge and a dictionary. Included in each word's listing is the pronunciation, part of speech, and definition.

1. **biweekly** (bī wēk′ lē) *adj:* **1.** occurring once every two weeks. **2.** occurring twice a week; semiweekly.

2. **bigamy** (big′ ə mē) *n:* the act of marrying one person while still being legally married to another

3. **bilingual** (bī ling′ gwəl) *adj:* **1.** written in two languages. **2.** able to speak two languages fluently.

4. **decade** (dek′ ād) *n:* a period of ten years.

5. **decimal** (des′ ə məl) *adj:* **1.** pertaining to tenths or founded on the number 10. **2.** proceeding by tens: *a decimal system.*

6. **demitasse** (dem′ i tas′, dem′ ē-) *n:* **1.** a small cup for serving after-dinner coffee. **2.** the coffee served.

7. **microphone** (mī′ krə fōn′) *n:* a device for transforming sound waves into changes in electrical current for recording or transmitting sound.

8. **microscope** (mī′ krə skōp′) *n:* an optical instrument used for magnifying objects too small to be seen by the unaided eye.

9. **millionaire** (mil′ yə nâr′, mil′ yə nâr′) *n:* a person whose wealth amounts to a million in dollars or some other currency.

10. **minicourse** (min′ ē kôrs) *n:* a course that is a shortened version of a regular-length course.

11. **miniature** (min′ ē ə chər) *n:* **1.** a small or reduced copy or model. *adj:* **2.** on or represented on a small or reduced scale: *a miniature dachshund.*

12. **minimum** (min′ ə məm) *n:* the least amount possible. **minimum wage**, *n:* the lowest hourly wage that may be paid to an employee.

13. **monopoly** (mə nop′ ə lē) *n:* **1.** exclusive control of a product or service that makes it possible to set prices. **2.** (*cap.*) a board game involving real estate properties bought with play money.

14. **monorail** (mon′ ə rāl) *n:* **1.** a single rail that serves as a track for railroad cars balanced on or suspended from it. **2.** a transportation system using such a rail.

15. **monotonous** (mə not′ ə nəs) *adj:* **1.** lacking variety; tediously unvarying in tone. **2.** uniform or repetitive.

16. **multitalented** (mul′ tē tal′ ənt ed) *adj:* possessing many special abilities or aptitudes.

17. **multiplex** (mul′ tē pleks′) *adj:* **1.** having many parts or aspects. *n:* **2.** a multiplex electronic system. **3.** a building containing a number of motion picture theaters.

18. **pentagon** (pen′ tə gon) *n:* **1.** a polygon having five angles and five sides. **2.** (*cap.*) a building in Arlington, Virginia, built in the form of a pentagon housing the U.S. Department of Defense.

19. **pentameter** (pen tam′ i tər) *n:* a line of verse or poetry consisting of five metrical feet.

20. **quad** (kwod) *n:* a quadrangle or court, as on a college campus.

21. **quadrilateral** (kwod′ rə lat′ ər əl) *adj:* **1.** having four sides. adj. **2.** *Geom.:* a four-sided polygon.

22. **quadruplet** (kwo drup′ lit) *n:* **1.** any group or combination of four. **2. quadruplets**, four children or offspring born at one birth.

23. **triceratops** (trī ser′ ə tops) *n:* a massive plant-eating dinosaur with a bony crest on the neck, a horn over each eye, and a horn on the nose.

24. **triple** (trip′ əl) *adj:* **1.** threefold; consisting of three parts. *n:* **2.** an amount, number, etc., three times as great as another. **3.** Also called *three-base hit:* a hit in baseball that enables a batter to reach third base safely. **4.** (in bowling) three strikes in succession.

25. **triple play** (trip′ əl plā′) *n:* a baseball play resulting in three putouts.

Exercise 1: Complete the Word

In the sentences below, select one of the prefixes to complete the underlined word. (More than one prefix may be correct.) Then write a definition for the word you have formed.

a. bi   d. micro   g. multi   i. quad
b. dec   e. mini   h. pent   j. tri
c. demi   f. mono

d   1. The lab partners quickly realized that their experiment with tiny specimens would require a ___ mi**cro**scope.

an optical

_e/g_   2. Evening students raved about the new _mini_ course in art history that would run on three consecutive nights at the college art museum.

_g_   3. After the new teacher received her class roster, she realized from the students' names the _multi_ cultural nature of her group.

_a_   4. James arranged to meet with his Spanish teacher on a _bi_ weekly basis until he caught up with the class.

_f_   5. The _mono_ rail system at Disneyland speeds tourists from one attraction to another and back to their hotels.

_i_   6. The new father, who had been expecting twins, was shocked to see his _quad_ ruplets born.

_b_   7. Juan found the transition from fractions to _de ci_ mals an easy one, as his teacher explained the two systems thoroughly.

_j_   8. The lead sports story on last night's news was the Yankees' game-winning _a tri_ ple play.

_h_   9. Before Sabrina could begin her job at the _pent_ agon, she had to submit a résumé and references from her former employer and congresswoman.

_c_   10. Joe always served his guests coffee in delicate _demi_ tasse cups.

Exercise 2: Select a Word

Use one of the words you have studied in this lesson to match the definition provided.

bilingual 1. able to speak two languages.

monopoly 2. a game whose object is for one person to own many properties.

triple 3. a hit in baseball that allows a player to reach third base.

minibus 4. a small bus usually used for short distances.

decade 5. a period of 10 years.

multiplex 6. a building containing many motion picture screens or theaters.

demitasse 7. an after-dinner coffee.

microphone 8. a device used to enlarge voice or sound for speaking or recording.

quad 9. an open courtyard on a college campus.

pentagon 10. a five-sided polygon.

Exercise 3: Use the Words in Context

In the following reading selection, you will find 10 numbered spaces. From the list of words that follows, select the word that fits best in each space.

After a ____1____ of raising children, Anita decided to begin a college education. In addition to desiring to start a career, she had begun to find her life as a housewife somewhat ____2____. She enrolled at a local community college and hoped that she would meet the ____3____ standards for acceptance into the liberal arts program. Her first week of class overwhelmed her. In her Spanish class, some of her classmates were ____4____, while she was trying to remember the vocabulary she once knew in high school. She found the sophisticated ____5____ in her chemistry lab difficult to use. In math, she felt comfortable with the ____6____ system but quite rusty with fractions. She felt comfortable only in her ____7____, *Introduction to College*, that met for one hour per week for the first five weeks of the semester. There she met other returning students who shared her anxieties. After class, they met in the _____8_____ for coffee and conversation. When Anita learned that others were neither smarter nor more confident than she, she started to believe in herself. Her counselor had asked Anita's professors to send _____9_____ progress reports, and, when the first ones arrived, they were glowing. In fact, one professor described Anita as a _____10_____ student whose contributions to class discussions were perceptive and welcome.

_____c_____ 1.   a. minicourse

_____h_____ 2.   b. biweekly

_____f_____ 3.   c. decade

_____d_____ 4.   d. bilingual

_____s_____ 5.   e. quad

_____g_____ 6.   f. minimum

_____a_____ 7.   g. decimal

_____e_____ 8.   h. monotonous

_____b_____ 9.   i. multitalented

_____i_____ 10.   j. microscope

Exercise 4: Use the Word Correctly

The sentences below contain underlined words that use the prefixes you have studied. Indicate whether the words are used correctly (C) or incorrectly (I).

_____C_____ 1. From studying the skeleton of the <u>triceratops</u>, scientists were able to draw some conclusions about the dinosaur's diet and habits.

_____C_____ 2. The math professor offered squares and rectangles as common examples of <u>quadrilaterals</u>.

_____I_____ 3. Arthur's arrest and <u>bigamy</u> charge were based on the discovery of the stolen money in his car.

_____C_____ 4. The Simpsons found the <u>monorail</u> at Disney World a convenient form of transportation.

I   5. As he ranted and raved about his players' poor performance, the coach tried to clarify what he expected as <u>mini-
mum</u> performance on the field.

C   6. The Smiths played <u>monopoly</u> whenever they traveled by
plane, since all they needed was a deck of cards.

C   7. To demonstrate the difficulty of writing certain types of
poetry, the English professor required his students to com-
pose a sonnet in iambic <u>pentameter.</u>

C   8. Several <u>decades</u> of unrestricted dumping led to contamina-
tion of the landfill and surrounding groundwater.

C   9. Maria enjoyed the variety of movie choices offered by the
new <u>multiplex</u> that opened in her town.

I   10. As a birthday gift, Melissa received a set of <u>miniature</u> china
that she planned to use to serve a Thanksgiving feast.

Exercise 5: Complete Analogies

Select the best word to complete each analogy.

a. minimum   c. multiply   e. quadruplet
b. monorail   d. pentagon   f. demitasse

b   1. highway : bus :: monorail : train
e   2. twin : quadruplet :: half-dollar : dollar
a   3. maximum : minimum :: plentiful : rare
c   4. divide : multiply :: subtract : add
f   5. demitasse : mug :: teaspoon : cup

g. minicourse   i. microphone   k. multimillionaire
h. quadriplegic   j. decade   l. triangle

i   6. voice : microphone :: star : telescope
l   7. triangle : square :: triple : home run
j   8. decade : century :: dime : dollar
g   9. chip : microchip :: course : minicourse
k   10. money : multimillionaire :: paintings : collector

ADDITIONAL PREFIXES 4

The prefixes you will learn in this chapter cannot be organized under a single category. They are, nevertheless, important because of their frequency. You will recognize some of them, and others will be new to you.

Prefix	Meaning	Examples
1. arch	chief, leader, ruler	archrival, monarch
2. auto	self	automatic, autonomous
3. bio	life	biology, biography
4. equi	equal	equilateral, equation
5. hetero	different	heterogeneous, heterosexual
6. homo	same	homogeneous, homosexual
7. manu	hand	manual, manicure
8. mis	wrong, error	mistake, misspell
9. para	at one side, beside	paralegal, paramilitary
10. sym, syn	same, with	symphony, synonym

WORD LIST

The words in the following list include the prefixes that you are studying in this chapter. Some of the words you have met as you reviewed the meanings of the prefixes and sample words. Others you will learn as you complete the exercises and the quiz for this chapter. Most of the words you will need to answer the questions are found in this list. You can also rely on your own word knowledge and a dictionary. Included in each word's listing is the pronunciation, part of speech, and definition.

1. **archenemy** (ärch′ en′ ə mē) *n:* a chief enemy.

2. **archbishop** (ärch′ bish′ əp) *n:* a bishop of the highest rank.

3. **autobiography** (ô′ tə bī og′ rə fē) *n:* a story of a person's life written by that person.

4. **autograph** (ô′ tə graf′) *n:* a person's signature, esp. a signature of a famous person for keeping as a memento.

5. **automatic** (ô′ tə mat′ ik) *adj:* **1.** able to start, operate, or move independently: **2.** involuntary; reflex. *n:* **3.** a machine or device that operates automatically; an automatic firearm. **4.** *Idiom:* **on automatic,** being operated or controlled by or as if by an automatic device.

6. **biodegradable** (bī′ ō di grā′ də bəl) *adj:* capable of decaying by natural biological processes: *biodegradable detergent.*

7. **biology** (bī ol′ ə jē) *n:* a science that deals with life or living matter in all its forms and processes.

8. **equalize** (ē′ kwə līz′) *v:* **1.** to make equal. **2.** to make uniform or constant.

9. **equation** (i kwā′ zhen) *n:* **1.** the act of equating or making equal. **2.** an algebraic expression designating the equality of two quantities.

10. **equivalent** (i kwiv′ ə lənt) *adj:* equal in value, measure, force, effect, or meaning.

11. **heterogeneous** (het′ ər ə jē′ nē əs) *adj:* **1.** different in kind; unlike. **2.** composed of dissimilar parts.

12. **heterosexual** (het′ ər ə sek′ shōō əl) *adj:* having or exhibiting a sexual desire for persons of the opposite sex.

13. **homicide** (hom′ ə sīd) *n:* the killing of one human being by another.

14. **homogeneous** (hō′ mə jē′ nē əs) *adj:* **1.** composed of parts or elements that are all of the same kind. **2.** of the same kind or nature; essentially alike.

15. **homosexual** (hō′ mə sek′ shōō əl) *adj:* attracted sexually to members of one's own sex.

16. **manual** (man′ yōō əl), *adj:* **1.** operated by the hands. **2.** made by hands as opposed to by machines. *n:* **3.** a small reference book with instructions.

17. **manufacture** (man yə fak′ chər) *v:* **1.** to make into a product, esp. as part of a big industrial process. **2.** to create or invent.

18. **misappropriate** (mis′ ə prō′ prē āt′) *v:* **1.** to put to a wrong use. **2.** to apply dishonestly, as funds entrusted to one's care.

19. **misfortune** (mis fôr′ chən) *n:* **1.** ill fortune; bad luck. **2.** a calamity or mishap.

20. **monarchy** (mon′ ər kē) *n:* government in which the supreme power is a monarch, as a king or queen.

21. **paralegal** (par′ ə lē′ gəl) *n:* an attorney's assistant trained to perform certain legal tasks but not licensed to practice law.

22. **paramilitary** (par′ ə mil′ i ter′ ē) *adj:* formed on a military pattern; designating an organization operating in place of, or as a supplement to, a regular military force.

23. **paraphrase** (par′ ə frāz) *n:* **1.** a restatement of the meaning of a text or passage; rewording. *v:* **2.** to express the meaning of something in a paraphrase.

24. **symbol** (sim′ bəl) *n:* **1.** something representing something else; emblem or sign. **2.** a letter, figure, or other mark designating a quantity or operation, as in mathematics.

25. **sympathy** (sim′ pə thē) *n:* **1.** agreement in feeling between people. **2.** the harmony existing between persons of like tastes or dispositions. **3.** the ability to share the feelings of another, esp. in sorrow or trouble; compassion.

Exercise 1: Complete the Word

In the sentences below, select one of the prefixes to complete the underlined word. Then write a definition for the word you have formed.

a. para   d. equi   g. bio   i. mon
b. hetero   e. homi   h. manu   j. mis
c. sym   f. auto

1. After years of _____ mis fortune, Brian felt that his luck had turned around when he won a scholarship.

    bad luck

_C_ 2. Her supervisor's genuine expression of _____*sym*pathy on the death of her mother surprised and touched Sonia.

_d_ 3. When Marisol discovered that her salary was not _____*equi*valent to that of the male computer programmers in her group, she sued her employer.

_a_ 4. On weekends, the _____*para*military group organizes training exercises and simulated skirmishes.

_e_ 5. Lorraine expected her new police assignment to be challenging when she was transferred from the juvenile division to _____*homi*cide.

_g_ 6. Environmentalists urge consumers to purchase products that are labeled _____*bio*degradable.

_f_ 7. Although _____*auto* matic reflexes may be damaged in an accident, physical therapists work with patients to try to regain some motor memory.

_b_ 8. After spending four years on an urban city campus, Frank looked for a _____*hetero*geneous neighborhood to provide the cultural diversity he enjoyed.

question wrong _____ 9. As family scandals, economic constraints, and public resentment grow, the British people have begun to re-examine the role of the mon*arch*y.

_h_ 10. Prison work programs that require only _____*manu*al labor are not as effective in preparing offenders for work after release as those that provide training.

Exercise 2: Select a Word

Use one of the words you have studied in this lesson to match the definition provided.

autobiography 1. a written account of one's own life.

paraphrase 2. to say or write something in similar, but not exactly the same, words.

misappropriate 3. to use funds improperly or dishonestly.

equivalent 4. having the same value.

archbishop 5. a bishop of the highest rank who presides over other bishops.

manufacture 6. to make or produce something.

heterogeneous 7. different in kind; having dissimilar elements.

autograph 8. someone's signature.

homogeneous 9. similar.

symbol 10. something that represents something else; a sign.

Exercise 3: Use the Words in Context

In the following reading selection, you will find 10 numbered spaces. From the list of words that follows, select the word that fits best in each space.

As he approached the age of 90, the retired musician decided to write his ____1____. Karl Weber began his research by examining records his grandmother had kept. From the beginning, she was very ____2____ to his musical ambitions, even when his parents discouraged him. Her scrapbooks included pictures of him from the time he was born until her death. She also saved his report cards and publicity about the performances he gave as a professional violinist. Karl was amazed to see a newspaper clipping about his first public performance at the age of nine. Although the reporter praised his playing, he ____3____ his name. (His grandmother considered these mementos more than ____4____ to the scrapbooks her sister kept of her grandson's sports successes.) Brochures advertising Karl's appearance with the Chicago ____5____ Orchestra were preserved by his grandmother, too. She even kept his earliest musical compositions that she had asked him to ____6____ for her. He also discovered pictures that were taken at the Weber family reunions that took place every decade. Looking at the faces of his brothers and cousins in the photos, representing a tremendous variety of personalities and occupations, he realized what a ____7____ group his relatives were. Recalling his own childhood and his busy schedule at the time his own children were young made Karl wonder if he shouldn't have tried to ____8____ the time he spent with his family with the time he spent on his career. He also recalled the fierce competition between himself and his ____9____ for first violin in the city orchestra. He wondered if he and Stephen might have been friends if they weren't so competitive. He also concluded, as he reviewed the course of his long life, that he had been blessed with talent and good health and had suffered few ____10____.

_____ 1.   a. misspelled

_____ 2   b. equalize

_____ 3.   c. equivalent

_____ 4.   d. misfortunes

_____ 5.   e. autobiography

_____ 6.   f. arch-rival

_____ 7.   g. sympathetic

_____ 8.   h. autograph

_____ 9.   i. heterogeneous

_____ 10.   j. symphony

Exercise 4:　Use the Word Correctly

The sentences below contain underlined words that use the prefixes you have studied. Indicate whether the words are used correctly (C) or incorrectly (I).

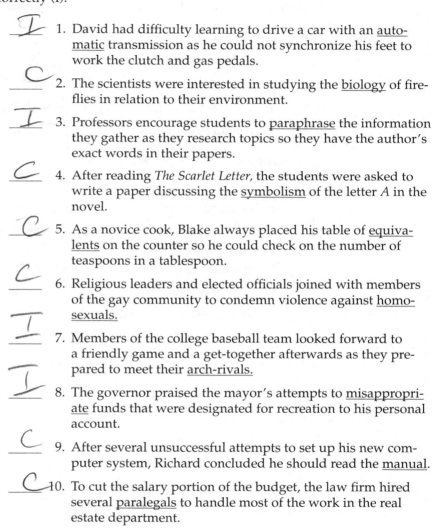

_I_　1. David had difficulty learning to drive a car with an <u>auto-matic</u> transmission as he could not synchronize his feet to work the clutch and gas pedals.

_C_　2. The scientists were interested in studying the <u>biology</u> of fire-flies in relation to their environment.

_I_　3. Professors encourage students to <u>paraphrase</u> the information they gather as they research topics so they have the author's exact words in their papers.

_C_　4. After reading *The Scarlet Letter,* the students were asked to write a paper discussing the <u>symbolism</u> of the letter *A* in the novel.

_C_　5. As a novice cook, Blake always placed his table of <u>equiva-lents</u> on the counter so he could check on the number of teaspoons in a tablespoon.

_C_　6. Religious leaders and elected officials joined with members of the gay community to condemn violence against <u>homo-sexuals.</u>

_I_　7. Members of the college baseball team looked forward to a friendly game and a get-together afterwards as they pre-pared to meet their <u>arch-rivals.</u>

_I_　8. The governor praised the mayor's attempts to <u>misappropri-ate</u> funds that were designated for recreation to his personal account.

_C_　9. After several unsuccessful attempts to set up his new com-puter system, Richard concluded he should read the <u>manual</u>.

_C_　10. To cut the salary portion of the budget, the law firm hired several <u>paralegals</u> to handle most of the work in the real estate department.

Exercise 5: Complete Analogies

Select the best word to complete each analogy below.

a. archbishop   c. biology   e. manual
b. paraphrase   d. symbol   f. equivalent

b 1. photograph : sketch :: copy : *paraphrase*

e 2. machine: hand :: automatic : *manual*

f 3. shy : outgoing :: *equivalent* : different

a 4. lieutenant : sergeant :: *archbishop* : bishop

c 5. criminology : crime :: *biology* : life

g. sympathy   i. heterogeneous   k. homicide
h. biodegradable   j. manufacture   l. archenemy

k 6. insecticide : bug :: *homicide* : person

i 7. anti-establishment : traditional :: homogeneous : *heterogeneous*

l 8. remember : commemorate :: arch-rival : *archenemy*

g 9. correction : mistake :: *sympathy* : apathy

j 10. error : mistake :: create : *manufacture*

COMMON ROOTS

The root is the heart of a word and is central to its meaning. In some cases, the root may form almost the entire word, as in the word *animal* (from the root *animus:* spirit). In other cases, the root may be surrounded by affixes, as in the word *encapsulate,* meaning to put something, like medicine, into a capsule (from the root *cap:* take or receive). Most of the time, you will need to know the root's meaning to figure out the definition of the word. Knowledge of prefix or suffix meanings will help, but usually will not be sufficient to figure out the entire word. Sometimes you will be able to piece together the meanings of the word parts to come up with the word's meaning, as:

en	+	cap	+	sul	+	ate
in		receive		(L. *capsula,* box)		verb forming suffix

You cannot just put the meanings of the word parts together and expect an automatic and sensible definition. "To receive in a box" makes some sense, but you can do better. With a little thought, and the clues above, you should be able to define the word *encapsulate* as meaning: to put something into a capsule, as medicine, or to summarize in capsule form, as a brief synopsis.

With other words, you will need to rely on context or additional information to determine the word's meaning, as:

un	+	sub	+	stan	+	tiated
not		under		stand		verb forming suffix (past tense)

The word *unsubstantiated* means not supported by proof or evidence. To arrive at this meaning, you would have to "play around" with the meanings of the word parts. You may think of the word *substance* and relate it to the context. For example, consider this sentence:

> The jury found the defendant not guilty because of unsubstantiated evidence.

You might use the clues "not guilty" and "evidence" to infer that the evidence was not good enough or was without substance. Literally, you might arrive at the same conclusion if you piece together the word parts to indicate that the charge "couldn't stand on the evidence" or there was not enough "under lying" support. As a reader, you should make use of **all** the clues available to you as you meet unfamiliar words: knowledge of word parts, background information about the word or topic, and context. If none of these work alone or in combination, resort to the glossary or the dictionary.

The following list contains 10 common roots, their meanings, and examples of words in which they are found. A word list follows; then, practice exercises allow you to define words that contain these roots, combine word parts, and use words correctly.

Root	Meaning	Examples
1. anima, animus	spirit, mind, soul	animated, magnanimous
2. cap, cep	take, receive	reception, capture
3. cura	care	cure, manicure
4. duc	lead	conductor, reduction
5. fug	flee	refugee, fugitive
6. loc	place	location, locomotive
7. naut	related to the sea	nautical, nautilus
8. phil	love of	philosophy, philanthropy
9. scope	see	telescope, microscope
10. tox	poison	toxin, nontoxic

Notes

1. The root *cap* also means head in certain words, as *capital* and *decapitate*. In this chapter, however, we will consider only its meaning of to take or receive.

2. The root *loco* has an alternative meaning that comes from Mexico. Eating certain plants, known as locoweed, can cause sheep or cattle to become ill. The disease is called *locoism* and is characterized by weakness, impaired vision, and irregular behavior. As a slang expression, the word *loco* is also used to describe people whose behavior is erratic or to refer to an insane or crazy person. In this chapter, we will restrict the root *loc* to its meaning of place.

WORD LIST

The words in the following list include the roots that you are studying in this chapter. Some of the words you have met as you reviewed the meanings of the roots and sample words. Others you will learn as you complete the exercises and the quiz for this chapter. Most of the words you will need to answer the questions are found in this list. You can also rely on your own word knowledge and a dictionary. Included in each word's listing is the pronunciation, part of speech, and definition.

1. **animate** (an′ ə māt) *v:* **1.** to give life to. **2.** to impart spirit or vigor. **3.** to make appear to move, as a cartoon figure.

2. **aquanaut** (ak′ wə nôt′) *n:* a scuba diver who works for an extended period of time underwater.

3. **astronaut** (as′ trə nôt′) *n:* a person engaged in or trained for space travel.

4. **bibliophile** (bib′ lē ə fil, -fīl) *n:* one who loves or collects books.

5. **captive** (kap′ tiv) *n:* a prisoner.

6. **conductor** (kən duk′ tər) *n:* **1.** a leader, guide, director, or manager. **2.** an employee on a bus or train who collects tickets, etc. **3.** a person who directs a band, orchestra, or chorus. **4.** a material that conducts heat or electricity.

7. **curator** (kyoo rā′ tər) *n:* the person in charge of a museum, art collection, zoo, etc.

8. **fugitive** (fyoo′ ji tiv) *n:* a person who is fleeing from prosecution, or running away from intolerable circumstances.

9. **locomotive** (lō′ kə mō′ tiv) *n:* a self-propelled engine for pulling a train or individual railroad cars.

10. **magnanimous** (mag nan′ ə məs) *adj:* **1.** generous in forgiving an insult or injury; free from pettiness. **2.** noble; generous.

11. **manicure** (man′ i kyoor′) *n:* treatment of the hands and fingernails.

12. **nautical** (nô′ ti kəl) *adj:* related to the sea, sailors, ships, or navigation.

13. **periscope** (per′ ə skōp) *n:* an instrument for viewing objects from a blocked view, used especially in submarines.

14. **philanthropist** (fi lan′ thrə pist) *n:* a person who is interested in the well-being of others; one who donates money, property, or work to needy persons or institutions.

15. **philosophy** (fi los′ ə fē) *n:* **1.** investigation of the truths and principles of human knowledge. **2.** the sum of the ideas and beliefs of an individual or group.

16. **receptacle** (ri sep′ tə kəl) *n:* **1.** a container that receives or holds something. **2.** the enlarged end of a flower. **3.** an electrical fitting.

17. **reception** (ri sep′ shən) *n:* **1.** the act of receiving. **2.** a welcome or acceptance. **3.** a social function when guests are formally received. **4.** the quality or fidelity in radio or television broadcasts.

18. **refugee** (ref′ yoo jē′) *n:* a person who flees for safety, esp. to a foreign country, for political reasons.

19. **toxemia** (tok sē′ mē ə) *n:* **1.** a blood poisoning. **2.** an abnormal condition of pregnancy characterized by hypertension, fluid retention, and edema.

20. **toxin** (tok′ sin) *n:* a poisonous substance produced by a living organism.

Exercise 1: Complete the Word

In the sentences below, select one of the roots to complete the underlined word. Then write a definition for the word you have formed.

a. anima   d. duc   g. naut   i. scope
b. cep   e. fug   h. phil   j. tox
c. cura   f. loc

_i_ 1. As part of her submarine training course, Rebecca's learned how to operate a peri scope .
an instrument of viewing objects from a blocked view.

_g_ 2. In addition to her career as an astro naut , Sally Ride also writes scientific books about outer space for children.
a person trained for space travel

_j_ 3. After several animals died mysteriously, the farmer called on a scientist to test for the presence of tox ins.
a poisonous substance produced by a living organism.

_a_ 4 When Ron completed his art degree, he decided to pursue a career in anima tion and applied for work at the Disney studio.
to give life to.

_c_ 5. As the new museum ___cura___tor, Jolanda's responsibilities included purchasing new acquisitions and organizing exhibits.

In charge of the museum

_h_ 6. Don's counselor analyzed his responses to an interest survey

and concluded that he was a biblio _phile_ e who should consider a career as a librarian.

one who loves or collects books.

_b_ 7. The law requires that all public buildings in the state pro-

vide separate re _cep_ tacles for trash and recyclable material.

a container that recives or holds something

_f_ 8. Rather than consulting a renowned physician at a university hospital, Steve chose to rely on his family doctor and a

___lo___cal hospital.

location or place

_d_ 9. The train con_ductor_ tor waited until all passengers were seated before he collected tickets.

an employee on a train who collects tickets

_e_ 10. Re_fug_ ees from the storm, the hikers discovered an abandoned cabin to provide shelter.

a person who flees for safety.

Exercise 2: Select a Word

Use one of the words you have studied in this lesson to match the definition provided.

manicure 1. professional care of the hands.

animated 2. lively.

toxin 3. a poisonous substance.

prisoner 4. imprisoned.

aquanaut 5. an undersea explorer or researcher.

phylosophy 6. the study of principles of being, knowledge, or conduct (literally, the love of wisdom).

periscope 7. a device used in submarines to look around the water surface.

fugitive 8. a person who is fleeing from prosecution; a runaway.

conductor 9. to lead or direct.

locomotive 10. railroad engine.

Exercise 3: Use the Words in Context

In the following reading selection, you will find 10 numbered spaces. From the list of words that follows, select the word that fits best in each space.

> Maria and Carlos began planning their wedding ceremony and ____1____ six months before the actual date. Since both of them come from large families and have many friends, a restaurant or hall with a large ____2____ was needed. They finally selected a neighborhood restaurant because of its familiarity, comfort, and convenient ____3____. The owner introduced the couple to Theresa, his energetic and ____4____ banquet manager whose enthusiasm and creative ideas made the planning stage fun. Since Carlos is a naval officer, Theresa suggested a ____5____ theme for the decorations. She sketched floral centerpieces in the shape of sailboats. When Maria mentioned that many guests would bring their small children, Theresa assured her that all the decorations and favors would be ____6____, so the parents need not be overly concerned about what the toddlers might put in their mouths. Theresa recommended a big band with a ____7____ experienced in wedding traditions, such as the couple's first dance, tossing the bouquet, and cutting the cake. The restaurant employed a wonderful baker, a Polish ____8____ who had owned her own commercial bakery before fleeing her native country about 10 years ago. Finally, since Theresa's ____9____ is that the bride should enjoy her own party, she insisted that Maria leave the last-minute details to her and arranged massage, ____10____, and hairdressing appointments for the morning of the wedding.

f ___ 1.   a. conductor

c ___ 2.   b. location

b ___ 3.   c. capacity

h ___ 4.   d. manicure

j ___ 5.   e. nontoxic

e ___ 6.   f. reception

a ___ 7.   g. philosophy

i ___ 8.   h. animated

g ___ 9.   i. refugee

d ___ 10.   j. nautical

Exercise 4: Use the Word Correctly

The sentences below contain underlined words that use the roots you have
studied. Indicate whether the words are used correctly (C) or incorrectly (I).

C ___ 1. Because of a fire in the <u>locomotive</u>, the train arrived two
hours late.

C ___ 2. Although his computer company had earned millions of dollars, the <u>philanthropist</u> never contributed to local churches
or community projects.

I ___ 3. The scientists studied the paths of several planets with the
high-powered <u>periscope</u>.

C ___ 4. Rather than telling the workers they were fired, the manager
announced a temporary <u>reduction</u> in force that would elimi-
nate certain positions.

C ___ 5. After snow caused the zoo's aviary roof to collapse, attempts
were made to <u>recapture</u> the birds before they died from
exposure.

C ___ 6. The floundering ship's captain reported his location as three
<u>nautical</u> miles from the number 20 buoy and requested
Coast Guard assistance.

C ___ 7. After her doctor concluded that Lisa was suffering from
<u>toxemia</u> in her fourth month of pregnancy, she ordered her
to bed.

_C_   8. Allison believed herself <u>cured</u> of the flu as she continued to run a high fever and vomit.

_I_   9. Hector's <u>magnanimous</u> spirit toward his in-laws became apparent as he continued to hold a grudge about their criticism of his business sense.

_C_ 10. The <u>conductor</u> acknowledged the audience's applause and invited the orchestra members to stand and share it with her.

Exercise 5: Complete Analogies

Select the best word to complete each analogy below.

a. receptacle   c. curate   e. periscope
b. animated   d. refugee   f. locomotive

_e_ 1. telescope : far :: *periscope* : around
_b_ 2. dull : *animated* :: toxic : nontoxic
_d_ 3. motorist : drive :: *refugee* : flee
_a_ 4. *receptacle* : hamper :: light : lamp
_f_ 5. engine : boat :: *locomotive* : train

g. captive   i. manicure   k. magnanimous
h. nautilus   j. aquanaut   l. animated

_j_   6. star : astronaut :: sea : *aquanaut*
_k_   7. homogeneous : heterogeneous :: *magnanimous* : petty
_g_   8. captor : *captive* :: hunter : prey
_l_   9. dull : *animated* :: shy : outgoing
_i_ 10. pedicure : foot :: *manicure* : hand

MORE ROOTS 6

As you continue to meet new words, you will recognize more of the word parts you have already learned. Notice that in the chapters on roots, many of the examples and words in the chapter word list contain prefixes you have studied in previous chapters. If you know the meanings of the root and the prefix, you have a significant head start in determining the word's meaning. Of course, you should always rely on context to add information or confirm your definition.

The following list contains 10 common roots, their meanings, and examples of words in which they are found. A word list follows; then, practice exercises allow you to define words that contain these roots, combine word parts, and use words correctly.

Root	Meaning	Examples
1. anthropo	human	anthropology, misanthrope
2. cede	yield	recede, secede
3. cycle	circle	bicycle, cyclical
4. fac, fic	make, do	factory, fiction
5. juv	young	juvenile, rejuvenate
6. luc, lum	light	illuminate, lucid
7. nov	new	novelty, novice
8. phono	sound	telephone, microphone
9. sphere	ball	atmosphere, hemisphere
10. view	see, look at	preview, viewer

Note
Do not confuse the root *nov*, meaning new, with the word part *novem*, which means nine, as in November (at one time, the ninth month of the year).

WORD LIST

The words in the following list include the roots that you are studying in this chapter. Some of the words you have met as you reviewed the meanings of the roots and sample words. Others you will learn as you complete the exercises and the quiz for this chapter. Not all of the words you will need to answer the questions are found in this list. You will also need to rely on your own word knowledge and a dictionary. Included in each word's listing is the pronunciation, part of speech, and definition.

1. **anthropology** (an′ thrə pol′ ə jē) *n:* the science that deals with the physical and cultural development, biological characteristics, and social customs and beliefs of human beings.

2. **atmosphere** (at′ məs fēr′) *n:* **1.** the gaseous envelope surrounding the earth or a heavenly body; the air. **2.** a unit of pressure; the normal pressure of the air at sea level, about 14.7 pounds per square inch. **3.** a psychological environment or pervading mood: *a friendly atmosphere.*

3. **concede** (kən sēd′) *v:* **1.** to acknowledge as true; admit, often grudgingly: *He finally conceded that she was right.* **2.** to acknowledge (an opponent's victory, score, etc.) before it is official: *to concede a match.* **3.** to yield; to grant as a right or privilege.

4. **cyclone** (sī′ klōn) *n:* a large-scale atmospheric wind-and-pressure disturbance characterized by low pressure at its center and circular wind motion.

5. **facsimile** (fak sim′ ə lē) *n:* **1.** an exact copy or reproduction. **2.** a system of transmitting images or printed matter electronically; often abbreviated as *fax.*

6. **fiction** (fik′ shən) *n:* **1.** the category of literature including works of an imaginative nature, such as novels or short stories. **2.** something invented, imagined, or made up.

7. **hemisphere** (hem′ i sfēr) *n:* **1.** one of the halves of the earth, usually divided at the equator into the Northern and Southern Hemispheres. **2.** a half of a sphere.

8. **illuminate** (i lo͞o′ mə nāt′) *v:* **1.** to light up. **2.** to make lucid, clarify. **3.** to decorate with lights.

9. **juvenile** (jōō′ və nil) *adj:* **1.** designed for young people: *juvenile books.* **2.** young, youthful. **3.** immature, childish, infantile: *juvenile behavior. n:* **4.** a young person, youth.

10. **lucid** (lōō′ sid) *adj:* **1.** easily understood: *a lucid explanation.* **2.** rational, mentally sound: *a lucid interval.* **3.** clear; transparent.

11. **luminous** (lōō′ mə nəs) *adj:* **1.** giving off or reflecting light; shining. **2.** clear; readily understood.

12. **megaphone** (meg′ ə fōn′) *n:* a cone-shaped device for amplifying the voice.

13. **misanthrope** (mis′ ən thrōp) *n:* one who hates humankind.

14. **novel** (nov′ əl) *n:* **1.** a long, fictitious prose narrative, portraying characters and having a plot. *adj:* **2.** of a new kind; different from anything seen or known before: *a novel idea.*

15. **novice** (nov′ is) *n:* **1.** a beginner; a person who is new to his or her circumstances, work, etc. **2.** a person admitted into a religious order or congregation for a period of probation before taking vows.

16. **phonics** (fon′ iks) *n: (used with a sing. verb)* a method of teaching reading and spelling based upon the sounds of letters and syllables.

17. **preview** (prē′ vyōō) *n:* **1.** an early or advance view, as an advance showing of a motion picture, play, etc. before its public opening. *v:* **2.** to view or show beforehand or in advance.

18. **recede** (ri sēd′) *v:* **1.** to move back to a more distant point; retreat; withdraw. **2.** to slope backward: *a receding shoreline.*

19. **rejuvenate** (ri jōō′ və nāt′) *v:* **1.** to restore to youthful vigor, appearance, etc.; to make young again. **2.** to restore to a former state; to refresh.

20. **review** (ri vyōō′) *n:* **1.** a critical article, as in a newspaper, about a book, play, performance, etc.; a critique. **2.** to study again; to memorize or summarize the facts. **3.** a formal inspection of a military or naval force group. **4.** a periodical containing articles on current affairs, books, art, etc.: *a literary review.* **5.** an examination, as by a higher court, of the decision in a case. *v:* **6.** to go over (lessons, studies, work, etc.) in review. **7.** to inspect, esp. formally: *to review the troops.* **8.** to survey mentally; examine: *review the situation.* **9.** to discuss (a book, play, etc.) in a critical review. **10.** to look back upon. **11.** to reexamine judicially: *to review a case.*

Exercise 1: Complete the Word

In the sentences below, select one of the roots to complete the underlined word. Then write a definition for the word you have formed.

a. sphere   d. anthro   g. cede   i. cycl
b. fic   e. view   h. lum   j. phone
c. juv   f. nov

_____ 1. At community meetings, residents discussed plans to halt beach erosion after the last major storm caused their shore

line to re_____ several feet .

_____

_____ 2. Indira enjoyed her _____pology course more than her psychology class because of its emphasis on groups rather than individuals.

_____

_____ 3. The _____ice plumber spent two years working under the supervision of his more experienced partner.

_____

_____ 4. As a biology major, Spencer spent most of his time reading textbooks and scientific journals, but he

preferred _____tion for recreational reading.

_____

_____ 5. An invitation to a pre_____ performance from the popular playwright pleased Ted who had tried unsuccessfully to buy opening night tickets.

_____

_____ 6. The organizer of the rally provided the first speaker with a

mega_____ so that the large crowd could hear her.

_____

_____ 7. Manuel's first trip to the Northern Hemi_____ left him longing for the warm temperatures of his homeland.

_____

_____ 8. A heavy caseload prevented the _____ enile probation officer from visiting his young clients as often as he
would have liked.

_____

_____ 9. On December 1, the mayor pulled the switch, and the huge

Christmas tree on the town green was <u>il_____ inated</u>
with red and green lights.

_____

_____ 10. On Michelle's first trip to the midwest, she was truly

amazed by the sight of a _____ one that had not
been predicted by the weather bureau.

_____

Exercise 2: Select a Word

Use one of the roots you have studied in this lesson to match the definition
provided.

_____ 1. the gaseous envelope surrounding the earth.

_____ 2. to make young again.

_____ 3. one who studies humankind and cultures.

_____ 4. a large scale storm with pressure at the center and
circular winds.

_____ 5. a building where goods are manufactured.

_____ 6. shining; lighted.

_____ 7. a state, quality, or object that is new.

_____ 8. instrument for speaking to someone at a distance.

_____ 9. to look over again.

_____ 10. to yield.

Exercise 3: Use the Words in Context

In the following reading selection, you will find 10 numbered spaces. From the list of words that follows, select the word that fits best in each space.

A group of environmentalists and ____1____ initiated a campaign to discourage people from adopting a view of the universe in which humans are the focus. Instead, they recommended looking at each ____2____ as a whole and exploring the interrelationships among creatures, plants, and their environments. They prepared brochures, posters, and learning packets that they asked elementary school teachers to ____3____ and comment on. In these packets, they suggested teachers help children imagine what the world was like in the time before industrialization and tremendous population growth. They ____4____ that it would be a difficult task with young children, but they also provided visual aids to help the teachers and children. Before the invention of ____5____ and ____6____, life was simpler and the ____7____ of nature played a more important role for people whose lives were closely connected with the land. Before electricity ____8____ homes, towns, and workplaces, the daily routine was tied to the rising and setting of the sun. Conscientious farmers left fields fallow periodically or rotated crops so the land could be ____9____ rather than relying on commercial fertilizers. While the environmentalists concede that some of the ____10____ methods of farming do have advantages, they also appreciate some of the old, traditional ways that may be more environmentally sensitive for the environment as a whole. Their goal is to persuade people, starting with the children, that if we try to foster an attitude that expresses concern for all living organisms, including humans, we may all benefit from a healthier and safer environment.

_____ 1.	a. cycle
_____ 2.	b. review
_____ 3.	c. illuminated
_____ 4.	d. anthropologists
_____ 5.	e. novel
_____ 6.	f. conceded
_____ 7.	g. hemisphere

_____ 8.   h. factories

_____ 9.   i. rejuvenated

_____ 10.   j. telephones

Exercise 4: Use the Word Correctly

The sentences below contain underlined words that use the roots you have studied. Indicate whether the words are used correctly (C) or incorrectly (I).

_____ 1. The cabin attendants distributed headsets to the airline passengers so that they could <u>view</u> the musical selections that were broadcast in flight.

_____ 2. The <u>luminous</u> paint dulled the finish on the getaway car so that potential witnesses to the robbery would have difficulty describing the vehicle.

_____ 3. The life of a deciduous tree is described as <u>cyclical</u> as it goes through a dormant period each winter and begins its growing stage each spring.

_____ 4. The persuasive saleswoman assured Marguerite that the vitamin enriched facial cream would erase her wrinkles and <u>rejuvenate</u> her appearance.

_____ 5. During his annual trip to Atlantic City, Seymour bet $25 at the casino and purchased <u>novelty</u> items for his grandchildren at a boardwalk shop.

_____ 6. Children who learn to read using the <u>phonics</u> method are told to rely on meaning and context to figure out new words.

_____ 7. Wilson earned his reputation as a <u>misanthrope</u> because of his ill temper and mean spirit.

_____ 8. When Barbara found herself unemployed after college, she <u>conceded</u> that her parents' advice to choose a practical major had been right.

_____ 9. Astronauts must wear special space suits if they expose themselves to the <u>atmosphere</u> during their missions.

_____ 10. The government order for 2,000 <u>manufactured</u> sheep delighted the Iowa farmer and convinced him that he would earn a profit for the year.

Exercise 5: Complete Analogies

Select the best word to complete each analogy below.

a. novel   c. concede   e. juvenile
b. atmosphere   d. unicycle   f. luminous

_____   1. traditional : _____ :: calm : hectic

_____   2. single : triple :: _____ : tricycle

_____   3. _____ : dull :: successful : struggling

_____   4. envelope : letter :: _____ : earth

_____   5. adult : _____ :: butterfly : caterpillar

g. misanthrope   i. review   k. phonograph
h. lucid   j. recede   l. factory

_____   6. compact disk player : _____ :: word processor : typewriter

_____   7. preview : _____ :: pre-test : post-test

_____   8. cook : kitchen :: manufacture : _____

_____   9. devil : angel :: _____ : philanthropist

_____   10. insert : delete :: propel : _____

SUFFIXES

A suffix is a word part that has meaning and appears at the end of a word. In general, suffixes tell more about the use of the word than its meaning. For example, the suffixes *or, er,* and *ist* tell that the word names a person. But you could not figure out the meaning of the word *conductor* (a person who conducts or leads) or the word *hypnotist* (one who puts others in a trance-like state) without additional clues. The meaning of a suffix, though, when used in conjunction with the context and knowledge of other word part meanings can be very helpful in figuring out meanings of unfamiliar words.

The following list contains 10 word parts that are suffixes and examples of how they are used. A word list follows; then, practice exercises allow you to define words that contain these suffixes, combine word parts, and use words correctly.

Word Parts	*Meaning*	*Examples*
1. able, ible	capable of, able to	respectable, sensible
2. ate	possessing	literate, considerate
3. ism	belief in, state or condition	communism, patriotism
4. ist	one who	geologist, hypnotist
5. ize	to make into	computerize, dramatize
6. ly	in a specified manner	affectionately, sparingly
7. ness	state of being, state or condition	quietness, boldness
8. or, er	one who	interrogator, teacher
9. tion, sion	state of being	interruption, sensation
10. tude	state of being	gratitude, multitude

WORD LIST

The words in the following list include the suffixes that you are studying in this chapter. Some of the words you have met as you reviewed the meanings of the suffixes and sample words. Others you will learn as you complete the exercises and the quiz for this chapter. Most of the words you will need to answer the questions are found in this list. You can also rely on your own word knowledge and a dictionary. Included in each word's listing is the pronunciation, part of speech, and definition.

1. **affectionate** (ə fek′ shə net) *adj:* tender, loving.

2. **communism** (kom′ yə niz əm) *n:* **1.** a social system of common ownership of goods and property. **2.** the Marxist philosophy of a classless society practiced for many years in the former Soviet Union and other countries.

3. **computerize** (kom pyoo′ tə rīz) *v:* **1.** to control by means of a computer. **2.** to install or provide with computers. **3.** to transfer a manual system of recordkeeping, etc. to computers.

4. **dramatize** (dra′ mə tīz) *v:* **1.** to adapt for a theatrical production. **2.** to present in a theatrical way.

5. **geologist** (jē ol′ ə jist) *n:* one who studies the history and formation of the earth and its structure, esp. through examination of rocks.

6. **gratitude** (grat′ ə tood) *n:* thankfulness; appreciation.

7. **hypnotist** (hip′ nə tist) *n:* one who is able to induce a trance-like state in which the subject is responsive to suggestions.

8. **intangibly** (in tan′ jə blē) *adv:* **1.** in a manner that is not capable of being touched. **2.** vaguely.

9. **interrogator** (in ter′ ə gāt ər) *n:* one who examines by formal questioning.

10. **interruption** (in tə rup′ shən) *n:* **1.** a break in the continuity. **2.** a breaking into another's conversation or speech.

11. **likeness** (līk′ nes) *n:* resemblance; copy; portrait.

12. **literate** (lit′ ər it) *adj:* **1.** able to read or write. **2.** well-read; educated; cultured.

13. **multitude** (mul′ tə tood) *n:* a great number.

14. **patriotism** (pā′ trē ə tiz əm) *n:* loyalty to one's country.

15. **possession** (pə zhesh′ ən) *n:* **1.** the act or fact of ownership. **2.** something that is owned, as one's property. **3.** the state of being dominated.

16. **quietness** (kwī′ ət nes) *n:* **1.** a peaceful or tranquil state. **2.** the absence of noise.

17. **respectable** (ri spek′ tə bəl) *adj:* **1.** worthy of high regard. **2.** decent; proper. **3.** of a reasonable size or quantity.

18. **reversible** (ri ver′ sə bəl) *adj:* **1.** able to be turned upside down or inside out. **2.** capable of being changed in direction or position.

19. **sparsely** (spars′ lē) *adv:* thinly spread or scattered.

20. **terminator** (ter′ mə nā tər) *n:* one who finishes, concludes, or puts an end to.

Exercise 1: Complete the Word

In the sentences below, select one of the suffixes to complete the underlined word. Then write a definition for the word you have formed.

a. able	d. ist	g. ness	i. tion
b. ate	e. ize	h. er	j. tude
c. ism	f. ly		

_____ 1. After many years of living under <u>commun</u>_____,
residents of the former Soviet republics faced many difficulties as they adjusted to new freedoms.

_____

_____ 2. Linda always responded <u>affectionate</u>_____
whenever her grandson asked her to read a story or play a game with him.

_____

_____ 3. In trying to persuade the board of trustees to

<u>computer</u>_____ the circulation system,
the librarian emphasized accessibility.

_____

_____ 4. To express her <u>grati</u>_____to her host family, the foreign exchange student presented them with a friendship quilt.

_____

_____ 5. Finding him to be an extremely <u>depend</u>_____
employee, the store manager assigned Terry to close out the cash registers each night.

_____

_____ 6. Charles hoped that his weekly visits to a

hypnot_____ would help him in his
attempt to give up smoking.

_____

_____ 7. Retiring after 25 years as a nurse, Consuela looked
forward to doing volunteer work that had nothing

to do with ill_____.

_____

_____ 8. Although she was not liter_____ in English when
she arrived in the United States, Syoong Cho studied hard
and was admitted to medical school.

_____

_____ 9. When he applied for the position of wait_____ the
restaurant owner told Patrick he lacked experience.

_____

_____ 10. Faced with one interrup_____ after another, Iliana
finally abandoned her attempts to complete her résumé.

_____

Exercise 2: Select a Word

Use one of the suffixes you have studied in this lesson to match the definition provided.

_____ 1. one who plays the violin.

_____ 2. to turn a novel into a play.

_____ 3. done or made without much expense.

_____ 4. a state of peace.

_____ 5. honored by others.

_____ 6. able to be worn on both sides.

_____ 7. a great crowd of people.

_____ 8. a state of joy.

_____ 9. one who leads an orchestra.

_____ 10. a questioner.

Exercise 3: Use the Words in Context

In the following reading selection, you will find 10 numbered spaces. From the list of words that follows, select the word that fits best in each space.

> Emily had spent weeks searching for a summer job when the librarian called to offer her part-time work helping to ____1____ the list of fiction volumes. With ____2____, she accepted and, in her mind, started to spend the paycheck she would receive on Friday. Although she considered herself a ____3____ person, Emily was amazed at the ____4____ of novels she had never heard of. As she typed in brief summaries of each book, she made notes of the ones she wanted to borrow. After her first day of work, she went home with a thriller about an apparently ____5____ businessman who secretly worked for a terrorist organization and was known by the code name "The ____6____." Reading through the ____7____ of the night into the early dawn, Emily returned her book to the library the next morning and was ready for another. Mr. Harvey, the assistant librarian, wondered why Emily seemed to be working so slowly. Her typing speed was impressive, and she wasn't bothered by many ____8____. Nevertheless, she had made little progress in inputting data. It only took Ms. Romero, the head librarian, a few hours to figure out what was going on. Not wishing to play the role of ____9____ of her new employee, Ms. Romero gently suggested that Emily spend her breaks and lunch hour compiling her reading lists so that she could devote her working hours to her job. Emily realized her mistake and appreciated the opportunity for a second chance. The rest of the day, she worked diligently and spent her free time adding to her own list. That night, she went home with a story about a ____10____ who persuaded his subjects to donate money to a fake charity.

_____ 1.   a. terminator

_____ 2.   b. hypnotist

_____ 3.   c. gratitude

_____ 4.   d. respectable

_____ 5.   e. computerize

_____ 6.   f. quietness

_____ 7.   g. multitude

_____ 8.   h. interruptions

_____ 9.   i. interrogator

_____ 10.   j. literate

Exercise 4: Use the Word Correctly

The sentences below contain underlined words that use the suffixes you have studied. Indicate whether the words are used correctly (C) or incorrectly (I).

_____ 1. The academic standards committee's decision to expel the student who had stolen test copies from her professor's office was final and <u>reversible</u>.

_____ 2. A single priest served seven different churches on the <u>sparsely</u> populated Yucatan peninsula.

_____ 3. After a separation of 10 years, the sisters recognized each other immediately because of the strong family <u>likeness</u>.

_____ 4. The producer of the public radio "read aloud" program for children and parents hired accomplished actors to <u>dramatize</u> the stories for the audience.

_____ 5. The <u>geologist</u> persuaded his subject to return to a scene from his childhood to help him remember something about his father's disappearance.

_____ 6. Hired as a police <u>interrogator</u>, Sergeant Doyle patrolled the streets on foot each evening.

_____ 7. Overcome with <u>gratitude</u>, Michelle learned that the president of her company planned to move the operation to Georgia and hire a new staff.

_____ 8. In order to finish her work on time, Michelle allowed her answering machine to take her messages to avoid further <u>interruptions</u>,

_____ 9. One of the signs of a <u>literate</u> society is the presence of libraries and bookstores.

_____ 10. Ted and Alan prepared a dozen sandwiches and bought two bottles of Coke to feed the <u>multitude</u> they had invited to the family reunion.

Exercise 5: Complete Analogies

Select the best word to complete each analogy below.

a. computerize	c. multitude	e. intangibly
b. interrogator	d. quietness	f. literate

_____ 1. concretely : specifically :: vaguely : _____

_____ 2. calculate : numbers :: _____ : data

_____ 3. celebration : disaster :: _____ : racket

_____ 4. scholar : study :: _____ : question

_____ 5. fluent : language :: _____ : books

g. interruption	i. gratitude	k. affectionate
h. sparsely	j. terminator	l. possession

_____ 6. coordinated : awkward :: _____ : hostile

_____ 7. commercial : program :: _____ : conversation

_____ 8. sympathy : pity :: _____ : thanks

_____ 9. obligations : rights :: heavily : _____

_____ 10. labor : work :: ownership : _____

WORD FAMILIES   8

After learning as many word parts as you have already studied, you are probably noticing similarities and relationships among words. Familiarity with the meanings of some common word parts can introduce you to a whole set of related words. When you try to define an unfamiliar word, it is often helpful to recall other words that include one or more of the same word parts. In the following exercises, you will be provided with a word part, its meaning, and several words in which it is found. You will be asked to use some of these words in sentences and define others.

Exercise 1:   Word Part: **bene**
                            Meaning: **good**

Notice that the definitions for all of the words relate to something positive.

Example	*Meaning*
a. benefit	an advantage.
b. beneficiary	one who receives something, often money, through a will.
c. benign	not malignant, as a tumor; kindly.
d. beneficial	helpful.
e. benediction	a blessing.

Select the letter of the word that best fits in the sentences below.

_a_   1. Stanley accepted the job not for the salary, which was quite low, but for the health ___benefit___

_c_   2. Test results indicated that Marta's cyst was ___benign___ and she would need no treatment.

_b_   3. As the ___beneficiary___ of his grandfather's estate, Mark inherited the 200-acre farm and all its animals and equipment.

_e_   4. At the end of the worship service, members of the congregation remained in their seats to await the minister's ___benediction___

_d_   5. At the math review session, the instructor told her students that working out the practice problems would be very ___beneficial___ for them.

_a_   6. Cheating on an exam may get a student through a difficult course, but it provides no ___benefit___ in the long run.

_b_   7. Heather's new company provided her with a life insurance policy for which she named her daughter as the ___beneficiary___

_____   8. The realtor assured her clients that the sorry state of the vacant property was the result of _____ neglect rather than vandalism.

From the context of the sentence and your knowledge of the word family, write a definition for the underlined word in the sentences below.

9. After serving as the college's chief benefactor for many years, Edward Cartwright was honored by having the new fieldhouse he had donated named after him.

   a person who give support

10. The pastor urged the members of the youth group to include time and money for benevolence, fund-raising, and recreation as they planned their program.

   charity

Exercise 2:

Word Part: **spec**
Meaning: **look; see**

Notice that the definitions for all of the words relate to watching.

Example	*Meaning*
a. spectacular	exciting; sensational.
b. spectacle	a public display.
c. inspect	to examine.
d. spectacles	a pair of eyeglasses.
e. spectator	a person who watches an event.

Select the letter of the word that best fits in the sentences below.

_d_ 1. Martha's grandchildren giggled every time she asked, "Where did I put my _spectacles_ ?"

_e_ 2. Thirty-five thousand _spectators_ viewed the international soccer match.

_b_ 3. At family weddings, Mike often drank too much champagne and made a _spectacle_ of himself.

_a_ 4. Edith was anxious to see the film after reading a _spectacular_ review in the Sunday newspaper.

_c_ 5. The Coast Guard officer stopped several fishing boats to _inspect_ their registration documents.

e   6. Sidelined because of his leg injury, the basketball guard did not enjoy his role as a *spectator* at the game.

a   7. After preparing and serving Melissa a *spectacular* gourmet meal, Tyrone presented her with a diamond engagement ring.

b   8. Fascinated by the activities going on in each of the circus's three rings, the child could not decide which *spectacle* to watch.

From the context of the sentence and your knowledge of the word family, write a definition for the underlined words in the sentences below.

9. The health <u>inspector</u> always checked to be sure the kitchen staff properly refrigerated the mayonnaise.

The person who examines

10. The interviewer asked the investment analyst to <u>speculate</u> about the future of the stock market in light of recent international trade agreements.

to reflect or to guess

Exercise 3:   Word Part: **dict**
                  Meaning: **say**

Notice that the definitions for all the words include the notion of words.

Example	*Meaning*
a. dictation	the act of saying something for recording by hand or machine.
b. diction	the choice or use of words or their pronunciation.
c. dictator	an absolute ruler; one whose word is law.
d. dictionary	a reference book containing an alphabetical list of words and information about them.
e. contradict	to say the opposite of what someone else has said.

Select the letter of the word that best fits in the sentences below.

_c_ 1. After the removal of the country's powerful _dictator_, the new government needed to deal with the effects of years of corruption

_b_ 2. Señor Medina's _diction_ was so perfect that his Spanish language students had to adjust to the accents of people they met in Spain.

_d_ 3. Martin found that even a _dictionary_ didn't help his poor spelling because he couldn't spell words well enough to look them up.

_e_ 4. As a typical adolescent, Justin seemed to _contradict_ everything his mother said.

_a_ 5. The company vice president refused to hire Stephanie as her executive secretary because she could not take _dictation_

_e_ 6. Marcia hoped her latest test scores would _contradict_ her teacher's fear that she might not pass the course.

_b_ 7. Most students in the public speaking class needed to work on confidence, but Ricardo was more interested in perfecting his _diction_

_d_ 8. Even though he had studied the language for years, Mark relied on his French–English _dictionary_ when he visited Paris.

From the context of the sentence and your knowledge of the word family, write a definition for the underlined words in the sentences below.

9. Sam returned to the office after dinner and dictated three letters into his <u>Dictaphone</u> for his secretary to type the following morning.

   a machine that records the dictation words

10. Weather forecasters <u>predicted</u> a fine holiday weekend with warm temperatures and sunny skies.

   to foretell

Exercise 4:   Word Part: **mort**
                              Meaning: **death**

Notice that the definitions for all the words have something to do with death.

Example	*Meaning*
a. mortuary	a place where dead bodies are kept or prepared for burial.
b. postmortem	happening after death; an examination of a dead body; an analysis of something that has already happened.
c. immortal	not subject to death; having everlasting fame.
d. mortician	an undertaker or funeral director.
e. mortality	the state or condition of being subject to death; the death rate of a particular population.

Select the letter of the word that best fits in the sentences below.

_____ 1. The devastating earthquake caused the hospitals and the _____ to be filled to capacity.

_____ 2. The mysterious deaths of several hundred cows prompted the rancher to request a _____ from his veterinarian.

_____ 3. Beethoven's _____ symphonies guaranteed his place in musical history.

_____ 4. The shadow of his own _____ pushed the elderly scientist to work long hours in the hope of finding a cure for the disease in his lifetime.

_____ 5. From the time her husband died until his burial, Dorothy found the _____ to be kind and helpful.

_____ 6. The sports commentator's _____ analysis of the football game lasted almost as long as the second half.

_____ 7. As a student of _____ science, Ralph took courses in embalming, business, and human relations.

_____ 8. The rulers of ancient Egypt hoped their monuments and elaborate preparations for their own deaths would allow

them to be _____.

From the context of the sentence and your knowledge of the word family, write a definition for the underlined words in the sentences below.

9. The bank officer told James that an additional $75 monthly payment would allow him to amortize his mortgage in 15 years instead of 25.

_____ *gradually extinguish* _____

10. When Gail arrived at the president's house dressed in a formal gown on the wrong night, she was too mortified to return for the actual party.

_____ *ashamed, humiliated* _____

Exercise 5:

Word Part: **gen**
Meaning: **type, kind**

Notice that the definitions for all the words deal with categories or groups.

Example	*Meaning*
a. gene	a part of DNA found in chromosomes that transmits hereditary traits.
b. genocide	the deliberate elimination of a particular group.
c. homogeneous	similar; of the same type, kind, or group.
d. generation	offspring in a particular step or age group in the line of descent.
e. genetics	the science or study of heredity.

Select the letter of the word that best fits in the sentences below.

_____ 1. Scientists specializing in _____ have been able to detect and correct certain medical conditions before a child's birth.

_____ 2. During a period of bitter tribal warfare, one group accused the other of attempted _____.

_____ 3. Living in a _____ neighborhood did not prepare Melanie for the cultural diversity of her college community.

_____ 4. The presence of a particular _____ is a predictor of a specific type of heart disease.

_____ 5. Claire felt closer to members of her mother's _____ than she did to her cousins who were closer to her own age.

_____ 6. At first, rumors of Hitler's _____ plan for the Jews were dismissed as impossible.

_____ 7. As a result of the school system's _____ grouping plan, the children in Ms. Patel's fourth-grade class were above-average students.

_____ 8. Doctors are experimenting with _____ therapy to prevent congenital birth defects.

From the context of the sentence and your knowledge of the word family, write a definition for the underlined words in the sentences below.

9. Sociologists believe that <u>gender</u> differences between men and women may be caused by cultural factors rather than biological ones.

_____

10. With the assistance of a helpful clerk in the Irish village's records office, Maureen was able to trace the <u>genealogy</u> of her family for six generations.

_____

MORE WORD FAMILIES   9

In this chapter, you will continue your study of word families. You will recognize some of the words from your earlier study of word parts. Try to see the relationship among all the words in each word family. Use what you know about familiar words to figure out the meanings of related unfamiliar words. Just as family resemblance exists in people, you will see similarities in related words as well.

Exercise 1:

Word Part: **ali**
Meaning: **other**

Notice that the definitions for all of the words relate to something apart or different.

Example	*Meaning*
a. alien	a foreigner; a stranger.
b. alienate	to put off; to distance oneself.
c. alias	a false name.
d. inalienable	cannot be removed or transferred.
e. alibi	a claim to have been elsewhere other than at a crime scene; an excuse.

Select the letter of the word that best fits in the sentences below.

___*a*___ 1. When Tiku arrived in this country from India to work as a chemist, she was admitted as a resident _alien_.

___*c*___ 2. The witness protection program provided the family with a new identity that included an _alias_, a home in a new state, and jobs.

___*b*___ 3. Steve has few friends because he _alienate_s people with his rude comments.

___*e*___ 4. The defendant's lawyer warned her client that an _alibi_ provided by a close relative carries less weight than one from a stranger.

___*d*___ 5. The American Revolution stemmed from the colonists' belief that they had been denied certain _inalienable_ rights.

___*a*___ 6. Those who believe in UFO sightings and landings theorize that _aliens_ from a distant planet may have landed on earth.

___*e*___ 7. Josh needed a quick _alibi_ when his mother asked him about the missing chocolate cake she had baked for the PTA meeting.

C—d 8. At the reading of grandfather's will, the family realized that
he had used an *alias* ~~~~ and a false birth certificate to
secure a job.

From the context of the sentence and your knowledge of the word family,
write a definition for the underlined words in the sentences below.

9. Professor Franklin introduced the abbreviation <u>et al.</u> and encour-
aged his students to use it after the first name when citing works
with several authors.

*Latin abbreviation et al. means
and others.*

10. In the United States, property owners have <u>alienable</u> rights that
allow them to transfer deeds to others.

*transferable to the ownership of
another*

Exercise 2:

Word Part: **duc**
Meaning: **lead**

Notice that the definitions for all the words have to do with guiding or
leading.

Example	*Meaning*
a. conduct	to guide, lead, manage, or control.
b. induction	the act of bringing someone into military service; the formal ceremony of accepting someone in an organization.
c. aqueduct	a channel or pipe designed to transport water.
d. deduction	the amount taken away or subtracted; a conclusion drawn by reasoning from the general to the particular.
e. duct	a tube, canal, or passage through which a liquid or gas is conveyed.

Select the letter of the word that best fits in the sentences below.

_d_ 1. The size of the tax _deduction_ taken from Tonya's first paycheck shocked her.

_a_ 2. The electrician completed the wiring and the _conduct_ work for the work for the school's new heating system during spring vacation.

_a_ 3. Winston's music teacher's invitation to _conduct_ the jazz band during the winter concert pleased and flattered him.

_c_ 4. In order to move water from the reservoirs upstate to the city, huge _aqueduct_s were constructed.

_b_ 5. Steve did not learn his first assignment until after his _induction_ into the Marines.

_a_ 6. Electrical engineering students quickly learned to distinguish substances that _conduct_ electricity from those that serve as insulators.

_b_ 7. After the National Honor Society _induction_ the members and guests enjoyed punch and cookies.

_e_ 8. Because of a blockage in the heating _duct_, Ms. Chen's classroom was much colder than the others.

From the context of the sentence and your knowledge of the word family, write a definition for the underlined words in the sentences below.

9. As guest <u>conductor</u> for the city orchestra, the maestro was invited to parties and dinners in his honor every night of his week-long visit.

_____

10. The construction of a large <u>viaduct</u> across the ravine delayed the opening of the new highway by two months.

_____

Exercise 3:   Word Part: **civ**
                   Meaning: **citizen**

Notice that the definitions for all the words relate to people in public roles.

Example	*Meaning*
a. civilian	a person not in military service.
b. civilization	a society with accomplishments in arts, sciences, etc.
c. civics	the study of citizenship and its rights and duties.
d. civil	relating to community life or the concerns of citizens.
e. civility	courtesy; politeness; good manners.

Select the letter of the word that best fits in the sentences below.

_c_ 1. Mr. Collier's _civic_ class tour to Philadelphia included a visit to see the Liberty Bell.

_d_ 2. Antoinette hoped that a high score on the _civil_ service test would help her secure a job in the post office.

_b_ 3. On his first visit to Italy, Joe was amazed by the remains of the Roman _civilization_

_a_ 4. Military personnel received different benefits and abided by restrictions that did not affect the _civilian_ workers on the base.

_e_ 5. After the outburst related to an old disagreement between brothers, _civility_ returned to the family reunion.

_c_ 6. Members of the school board refused to hear arguments in favor of reducing the number of _civics_ courses required for graduation.

_d_ 7. During the 1960s, the _civil_ rights movement drew attention to the discrimination blacks had long experienced in this country.

b   8. Archaeologists have found indications that the Mayan
civilization had developed an alphabet and mathematical system.

From the context of the sentence and your knowledge of the word family, write a definition for the underlined words in the sentences below.

9. Amanda picked up her 12-year old son after a summer of camping and backpacking and realized she had to <u>civilize</u> him before school started.

_____

10. Guy arrived at the <u>civic</u> center three hours before the box office opened to buy tickets for the rock concert.

_____

Exercise 4:   Word Part: **mit or mis**
                       Meaning: **send**

Notice that the definitions for all the words have to do with conveying something.

Example	*Meaning*
a. transmit	to send from one person or place to another.
b. remission	pardon or relief from a penalty, debt, or disease.
c. commit	to do or perform; to entrust; to pledge oneself.
d. mission	a task, assignment, or obligation.
e. intermittent	stopping and starting.

Select the letter of the word that best fits in the sentences below.

_C_ 1. Unsure of how much time he could _Commit_ to the project, Lee refused the nomination to chair the task force.

_e_ 2. During the marathon, the _Intermitten_ rain provided the runners with a welcome relief from the heat.

_d_ 3. Sally Ride's first space _mission_ proved as exciting as she had hoped it would be.

_a_ 4. Telephone lines were run between headquarters and the battle stations so the troops could _transmit_ news of their progress.

_b_ 5. Two months after her last chemotherapy treatment, Sandra's doctor announced that her cancer was in _remission_

_a_ 6. An early breakthrough for Thomas Edison was his ability to _transmit_ a message from one room to another.

_d_ 7. Theresa felt it her _mission_ in life to persuade her father to stop smoking.

_c_ 8. James and Chris wrote their own wedding vows, promising to love, honor, and _commit_ themselves to one another.

From the context of the sentence and your knowledge of the word family, write a definition for the underlined words in the sentences below.

9. The offer for a "free" poster included the requirement to <u>remit</u> $3 for postage and handling.

_____

10. Luke's church required that he spend one year performing <u>missionary</u> work.

_____

Exercise 5:   Word Part: **cent**
                           Meaning: **hundred**

Notice that the definitions for all the words have to do with the number 100.

Example	*Meaning*
a. century	a period of one hundred years.
b. cent	a subdivision of a dollar, worth 1/100th.
c. centipede	a wormlike animal having many pairs of legs.
d. bicentennial	a two-hundred year anniversary celebration.
e. centimeter	a unit of measure equal to 1/100 of a meter.

Select the letter of the word that best fits in the sentences below.

_*b*_ 1. Stan set the price for his old car at $1,500 and said he would not accept one ___*cent*___ less.

_*d*_ 2. As part of the _bicentennial_ festivities, tall ships sailed into New York Harbor on the Fourth of July.

_*c*_ 3. After capturing a frog and announcing he planned to keep it for a pet, Matthew searched the garden but found only one _____ for food.

_*a*_ 4. At the turn of the _____, a feeling of the beginning of a new and modern age swept across the country.

_*e*_ 5. Specifications for the new experimental equipment were so precise that an error of even one _____ was unacceptable.

_____ 6. Colonists who arrived in America in the seventeenth _____ were often unprepared to face the harsh winters.

C   7. Although harmless, their prehistoric appearance makes

_____s unappealing to most people.

e   8. To complete her math assignment of conversions, Sarah
needed a ruler that indicated measurements in both inches

and _____s.

From the context of the sentence and your knowledge of the word family,
write a definition for the underlined words in the sentences below.

9. On her visit to Canada, Louise tried to adjust to the morning
weather report that told the temperature in centigrade.

_____

10. A morning talk-show host sends happy birthday wishes to any
centenarian whose picture and birth date are sent to the station.

_____

How to Use a Dictionary

10

Many good dictionaries are available for use and purchase. Depending on your purposes, you may choose to consult your college library's very large and complete dictionary, or you may rely on your own pocket dictionary. Many of you will be working with word-processing programs that provide some dictionary services. In fact, you will find it much easier to check your spelling using a word processor than a dictionary. With a dictionary, you need to have an approximate idea of the word's spelling to find it. A word processor's spell checker provides you with several words that are close to what you typed. If your version is close enough, all you have to do is recognize the correct word. It is the writer's responsibility, though, to make sure the chosen word makes sense. Students have been known to choose *jungle* and *jaguar* instead of *jugular,* resulting in a very confusing essay. You may also be able to use a thesaurus provided by your word processor. It shows you a list of synonyms for a particular word. If you need pronunciation, complete definitions, multiple meanings, or word origins, however, go to the dictionary.

All dictionaries include an introduction, guide, or "how to use" section at the beginning of the text. These are filled with useful information that tells you what you can learn about each word and how to find what you are looking for. Most people skip this section and go directly to the word in question. Some people who have had the same dictionary for years have no idea what it includes. Some examples are conversion tables for weights and measures, proofreaders' marks, the meanings of common given names, and guides for writers. You may wish to compare dictionaries before purchasing one. It would also be interesting to compare your dictionary with those of fellow students to see how they differ.

This chapter will give you a general idea of what is included in most dictionaries and some suggestions about how to use them. It is not tied to any particular dictionary, so the details may be slightly different in your particular edition. For the most part, though, dictionaries are generally set up the way they are described here, and you will be able to apply the suggestions for use to your dictionary.

Look at the sample entry below:

> **triv•i•al** (triv′ē əl) *adj:* 1. Of little importance or value. 2. Commonplace; ordinary; that which is found everywhere. [<L *trivialis* of the crossroads, commonplace < *tri-* three + *via-* road] — **triv′i•al•ism** *n.*
> — **triv′i•al•ly** *adv.*

Notice the following information:

triv•i•al   The word is spelled correctly, with dots to indicate divisions between syllables.

(triv′ē əl)   The correct pronunciation is provided. Each dictionary includes a pronunciation key at the beginning of the text. Some include an abbreviated version at the bottom of every double page. There is no need to memorize a pronunciation key, but there are some common symbols that would be useful to know. For short vowels, a small half moon or circle may be placed above the letter, or the letter may be written with no symbol. For long vowels, a straight line is usually placed above the letter, or the letter may be printed in **boldface type**. The schwa, ə, is a very common sound in the English language. It has the sound of "uh" and can be made by any vowel. Examples include the *a* in *above*, the *e* in *system*, and the *u* in *circus*. The stress mark ′ indicates which syllable has the greatest stress, emphasis, or loudness.

adj.   The part of speech is indicated. This tells you how the word will be used in a sentence.

1. Of little importance or value.
   Definitions are provided, with the most common one or the earliest known definition given first. Sometimes the first definition is just a variation of the word itself. (For example, the first definition for the word *induction* may be: 1. *the act of inducing.* To determine a useful meaning, you may have to consult the second meaning: 2. *formal installation in an office.*)

2. Commonplace; ordinary; that which is found everywhere.

> Many words have multiple meanings. In the present case, definitions 1 and 2 are quite similar. In other cases, the different meanings may be quite different. Think of the word *reception*. It could be used to indicate a party after a wedding, the way a new movie was evaluated, or the quality of a television signal.

[<L *trivialis* of the crossroads, commonplace < *tri*- three + *via*- road]

> The origin, derivation, and historical development—that is, the *etymology* of the word—is provided. In this case, we are told that the word *trivial* comes from the Latin word *trivialis*, which is itself made up of two other word parts: *tri* and *via*. Some dictionaries may also include additional information about the word's origin. In the case of *trivial*, in Roman times, places where three roads came together were often busy and accessible to all. In some cases, a bulletin board was placed there so people could leave messages for one another. Of course, you would not post an important or private message for all to see, so the messages were considered *trivia*.

— **triv′i•al•ism** *n.* — **triv′i•al•ly** *adv.*

> These are derived entries or closely related words that are usually different parts of speech. They are alternate forms of the entry word. In the case of verbs, they may be different tenses. If the entry word is a noun, the plural form may be listed.

Now look at the sample dictionary page. (*The American Heritage Dictionary of the English Language*, paperback edition, p. 414.) Notice that guide words are provided at the top of the page to indicate alphabetically the words that are included on this page. Notice also that a pronunciation key is included at the bottom of the page. Use this key, the entries, and the information you have just reviewed to answer the following questions about the words on this page.

loathsome / loft   **414**

loath•some (lōth′səm, lôth′-) *adj.* Abhorrent; repulsive; disgusting. —**loath′some•ly** *adv.*

loaves. *pl.* of **loaf¹.**

lob (lŏb) *v.* **lobbed, lobbing.** To hit, toss, or propel (something) slowly in a high arc. —*n.* A ball thus hit or thrown. [Prob < LG.]

lob•by (lŏb′ē) *n., pl.* **-bies.** 1. A hall, foyer, or waiting room in a hotel, apartment house, or theater. 2. A group of private persons engaged in influencing legislation. —*v.* **-bied, -bying.** To seek to influence legislators in favor of some special interest. [ML *lobium,* a monastic cloister.] —**lob′by•ism′** *n.* —**lob′by•ist** *n.*

lobe (lōb) *n.* 1. A rounded projection, esp. an anatomical part. 2. A structurally bounded subdivision of an organ or part. [< Gk *lobos.*] —**lo′bar** *adj.*

lo•bot•o•my (lō-bŏt′ə-mē, lə-) *n., pl.* **-mies.** Surgical incision into a lobe, esp. one in the brain.

lob•ster (lŏb′stər) *n.* 1. A large, edible marine crustacean with five pairs of legs, of which the first pair is large and clawlike. 2. Any of several related crustaceans. [< L *locusta,* locust, lobster.]

lo•cal (lō′kəl) *adj.* 1. Of or relating to a place. 2. Pertaining to, existing in, or serving a locality: *local government.* 3. Of or affecting a limited part of the body. 4. Making many stops: *a local train.* —*n.* 1. A public conveyance that stops at all stations. 2. A local branch of an organization, esp. of a labor union. [< L *locus,* place, LOCUS.] —**lo′cal•ly** *adv.*

lo•cale (lō-kăl′, -kăl′) *n.* A locality, with reference to some event.

lo•cal•i•ty (lō-kăl′ə-tē) *n., pl.* **-ties.** 1. A neighborhood, place, or district. 2. A site, as of an event.

lo•cal•ize (lō′kə-līz′) *v.* **-ized, -izing.** To confine or restrict to a particular area or part.

lo•cate (lō′kāt, lō-kāt′) *v.* **-cated, -cating.** 1. To determine the position of: *locate Albany on the map.* 2. To find by searching: *locate the source of error.* 3. To station, situate, or place. [< L *locus,* place, LOCUS.] —**lo′ca•tor** *n.*

lo•ca•tion (lō-kā′shən) *n.* 1. A place where something is located. 2. A site away from the grounds of a motion-picture studio, where a scene is shot: *make a movie on location.*

loc. cit. In the place cited (L *locō citātō*).

loch (lŏкн, lŏk) *n. Scot.* 1. A lake. 2. An arm of the sea similar to a fjord. [< Scot Gael.]

lo•ci. *pl.* of **locus.**

lock¹ (lŏk) *n.* 1. A key- or combination-operated mechanism used to secure a door, lid, etc. 2. A section of a canal closed off with gates for the purpose of raising or lowering the water level. 3. A mechanism in a firearm for exploding its charge of ammunition. —*v.* 1. To fasten or become fastened with a lock. 2. a. To confine or safeguard by putting behind a lock. b. To put in jail (with *up*). 3. To clasp or embrace tightly. 4. To entangle in struggle or battle. 5. To become entangled; interlock. 6. To jam or force together so as to make unmovable. 7. To become rigid or unmovable. [< OE *loc.*] —**lock′less** *adj.*

lock² (lŏk) *n.* 1. A strand or curl of hair. 2.

locks. The hair of the head. [< OE *locc.*]

lock•er (lŏk′ər) *n.* An enclosure that can be locked, esp. one in a gymnasium or public place, for the safekeeping of clothing and valuables.

lock•et (lŏk′ĭt) *n.* A small ornamental case for a picture or keepsake, usually worn as a pendant.

lock•jaw (lŏk′jô′) *n. Path.* 1. Tetanus. 2. A symptom of tetanus, in which the jaw muscles go into spasm.

lock•out (lŏk′out′) *n.* The closing down of a plant by an employer to coerce the workers into meeting his terms.

lock•smith (lŏk′smĭth′) *n.* One who makes or repairs locks.

lo•co (lō′kō) *adj. Slang.* Mad; insane. [< Span.]

lo•co•mo•tion (lō′kə-mō′shən) *n.* The act of moving or ability to move from place to place. [< L *locus,* place, LOCUS + MOTION.]

lo•co•mo•tive (lō′kə-mō′tĭv) *n.* A self-propelled engine that moves railroad cars. —*adj.* Of or involved in locomotion.

lo•co•weed (lō′kō-wēd′) *n.* Any of several W American plants that are poisonous to livestock.

lo•cus (lō′kəs) *n., pl.* **-ci** (-sī′). 1. A place. 2. The set or configuration of all points satisfying geometric conditions. [L *locus,* place.]

lo•cust¹ (lō′kəst) *n.* 1. A grasshopper that travels in destructive swarms. 2. A cicada. [< L *lōcusta,* locust, lobster.]

lo•cust² (lō′kəst) *n.* A tree with featherlike compound leaves and clusters of fragrant white flowers.

lo•cu•tion (lō-kyōō′shən) *n.* 1. A particular word, phrase, or expression. 2. Style of speaking; phraseology. [< L *loqui* (pp *locūtus*), to speak.]

lode (lōd) *n.* A vein of mineral ore deposited between layers of rock. [< OE *lād,* course, way. See **leith-.**]

lode•star (lōd′stär′) *n.* A star that is used as a point of reference, esp. the North Star. [ME *loode sterre,* "guiding star."]

lode•stone (lōd′stōn′) *n.* A magnetized piece of magnetite.

lodge (lŏj) *n.* 1. A cottage or cabin used as a temporary abode by a caretaker, gatekeeper, etc. 2. An inn. 3. a. A local chapter of certain fraternal organizations. b. The meeting hall of such a society. —*v.* **lodged, lodging.** 1. To provide with or rent quarters temporarily, esp for sleeping. 2. To live in a rented room or rooms. 3. To register (a charge): *lodge a complaint.* 4. To vest (authority or power). 5. To be or become embedded. [< OF *loge,* shed, small house.] —**lodge′a•ble** *adj.*

lodg•er (lŏj′ər) *n.* One who rents and lives in a furnished room or rooms; roomer.

lodg•ing (lŏj′ĭng) *n.* Often **lodgings.** Sleeping accommodations.

Łódź (lōōj). A city of C Poland. Pop. 700,000.

loft (lôft, lŏft) *n.* 1. A large, usually unpartitioned floor over a commercial building. 2. An open space under a roof; attic. 3. A gallery or balcony, as in a church: *a choir loft.*

ă pat/ā ate/âr care/ä bar/b bib/ch chew/d deed/ĕ pet/ē be/f fit/g gag/h hat/hw what/ ĭ pit/ī pie/îr pier/j judge/k kick/l lid, fatal/m mum/n no, sudden/ng sing/ŏ pot/ō go/

Exercise 1: Pronunciation

Write your answers to the following questions in the spaces provided.

_____ 1. Does the *o* in the word *lobe* have the same sound as the *o* in the word *loft*?

_____ 2. What sound does the *y* in the word *lobby* have?

_____ 3. Which syllable in the word *locomotion* is most stressed?

_____ 4. Are the words *local* and *locale* pronounced the same?

_____ 5. Do the words *lob* and *lobe* have the same pronunciation?

_____ 6. What letters in the words *lobotomy* and *locality* have the schwa sound?

_____ 7. What word does the second syllable in the word *locution* sound like?

_____ 8. What letters in the word *lodge* are silent?

_____ 9. Some words can be pronounced more than one way. Find two words for which there are two pronunciations provided.

_____ 10. Is the pronunciation of the insect *locust* the same as the *locust* tree?

Exercise 2: Meanings

Write your answers to the following questions in the spaces provided.

_____ 1. If you were taking a speech course, would you study *locomotion* or *locution*?

_____ 2. Which definition of the word *lobby* would you use to describe people hired by the National Rifle Association to dissuade lawmakers from passing gun control laws?

_____ 3. Which is a symptom of a serious infection: *lockjaw*, *lockout*, or *locksmith*?

_____ 4. What word can be used to identify a train that makes many stops?

_____   5. What does *loci* mean? (Don't just give its singular form. Figure out its definition.)

_____   6. Which definition of the word *lock* would you use if you were talking about a boat traveling on the inland waterway?

_____   7. If you were navigating a ship, would you use a *lodestar* or a *lodestone?*

_____   8. Which word would be used to describe the lower part of an ear?

_____   9. In a game of tennis, what shot would you hit if your opponent is right up at the net?

_____   10. Would a farmer be concerned about the threat from *lobsters* or *locusts?*

Exercise 3: Parts of Speech and Derived Entries

Write your answers to the following questions in the spaces provided.

_____   1. What would you call a person who is engaged in lobbying activities?

_____   2. What two parts of speech can the word *lock* be?

_____   3. What is the plural of *lobotomy?*

_____   4. Which entry is a proper noun, or a specific name?

_____   5. What would you call a person who finds or locates something, as a job or an apartment?

_____   6. Which word is a slang expression meaning crazy?

_____   7. Which entry is an abbreviation?

_____   8. What word is often used in its plural form to mean the same thing?

_____   9. What is the past tense of *localize?*

_____   10. What adverb comes from the word *loathsome?*

Exercise 4: Etymology

The following abbreviations are found on the sample page. They are listed below along with the language they stand for.

GK-	Greek
L-	Latin
LG-	Late Greek
ML-	Medieval Latin
OE-	Old English
OF-	Old French
Scot Gael-	Scottish
Span-	Spanish

Write your answers to the following questions in the spaces provided.

_____ 1. From what language do the words *lob* and *lobe* come?

_____ 2. What Latin word do *locale, locate,* and *locomotion* share as a source?

_____ 3. What other word has the same Latin derivation as *lobster*? Can you imagine why?

_____ 4. Do the two separate entries for the word *lock* share the same derivation?

_____ 5. What is the derivation of the word *lodge*?

_____ 6. In what country would you find a *loch*?

_____ 7. What does the Latin phrase *loode sterre* mean?

_____ 8. Where does the word *lode* come from?

_____ 9. Which is the only word on this page derived from Spanish?

_____ 10. From what Latin word does our word *locution* come?

Exercise 5: General Dictionary Skills

_____ 1. Would you find the word *liquidate* on this page, an earlier page, or a later page?

_____ 2. How would you find the meaning of the word *loaves*?

_____ 3. With what field of study is *lockjaw* associated?

_____ 4. Would you find the word *loiter* on this page, an earlier page, or a later page?

_____ 5. Where would you look for the meaning of the word *loci*?

ANSWERS TO EXERCISES

CHAPTER 1

Check your answers for the exercises in Chapter 1.

Exercise 1 - Complete the Word

1.	b	antecedents:	a previous word that a pronoun refers to
2.	j	sequel:	a follow-up work
3.	i	semicircle:	a half circle
4.	f	postpone:	to put off or delay
5.	c	archeologist:	a person who studies ancient cultures
6.	d	abbreviations:	shortened version of words
7.	a	annual:	occurring once a year
8.	g	preliminary:	introductory
9.	e	chronological:	in time order
10.	h	reproduced:	copied

Exercise 2 - Select a Word

1. archeology
2. sequel
3. rearrange
4. synchronize
5. consequence
6. abbreviation
7. semicolon
8. preliminary
9. postpone
10. anniversary

Exercise 3 - Use the Words in Context

1. c
2. g
3. d
4. h
5. f
6. e
7. j
8. a
9. i
10. b

Exercise 4 - Use the Word Correctly

1. C
2. I
3. C
4. C
5. I
6. I
7. C
8. I
9. C
10. I

Exercise 5 - Complete Analogies

1. f
2. d
3. a
4. e
5. b
6. j
7. l
8. h
9. k
10. i

CHAPTER 2

Check your answers for the exercises in Chapter 2.

Exercise 1 - Complete the Word

1.	h	promote:	sell; encourage the popularity of
2.	c	diagnosis:	identification of the problem or illness
3.	j	transport:	send
4.	g	primary:	beginning, early, or elementary
5.	e	epidermis:	outer layer of skin
6.	i	telecommunication:	the study of sending information or entertainment over distances
7.	b	circumvent:	avoid or get around
8.	a	centralize:	bring together under one head
9.	d	engrave:	carve or etch
10.	f	immerse:	submerge or plunge under water

Exercise 2 - Select a Word

1. epoxy
2. egocentric
3. transmit
4. diameter
5. circumstance
6. implant
7. propel
8. enclose
9. primer
10. circumference

Exercise 3 - Use the Words in Context

1. i
2. j
3. c
4. a
5. h
6. d
7. g
8. e
9. b
10. f

Exercise 4 - Use the Word Correctly

1. I
2. C
3. C
4. C
5. I
6. C
7. I
8. I
9. C
10. C

Exercise 5 - Complete Analogies

1. f
2. d
3. e
4. c
5. b
6. j
7. i
8. l
9. g
10. k

CHAPTER 3

Check your answers for the exercises in Chapter 3.

Exercise 1 - Complete the Word

1.	d	microscope:	an instrument used to make small things appear larger
2.	e	minicourse:	a shortened version of a course
3.	g	multicultural:	representing many different cultures
4.	a	biweekly:	twice a week or once every two weeks
5.	f	monorail:	a railroad system where the train cars ride on a single rail
6.	i	quadruplets:	four children born from the same pregnancy
7.	b	decimal:	number system based on tens
8.	j	triple play:	a baseball play that results in three outs
9.	h	pentagon:	five-sided building that houses the Dept. of Defense
10.	c	demitasse:	after-dinner coffee served in small cups

Exercise 2 - Select a Word

1. bilingual
2. monopoly
3. triple
4. minibus
5. decade
6. multiplex
7. demitasse
8. microphone or megaphone
9. quadrangle
10. pentagon

Exercise 3 - Use the Words in Context

1. c
2. h
3. f
4. d
5. j
6. g
7. a
8. e
9. b
10. i

Exercise 4 - Use the Word Correctly

1. C
2. C
3. I
4. C
5. C
6. I
7. C
8. C
9. C
10. I

Exercise 5 - Complete Analogies

1. b
2. e
3. a
4. c
5. f
6. i
7. l
8. j
9. g
10. k

CHAPTER 4

Check your answers for the exercises in Chapter 4.

Exercise 1- Complete the Word

1.	j	misfortune:	bad luck
2.	c	sympathy:	compassion
3.	d	equivalent:	of the same value
4.	a	paramilitary:	unofficial, military-like group
5.	e	homicide:	murder
6.	g	biodegradable:	able to decompose naturally
7.	f	automatic:	able to work independently
8.	b	heterogeneous:	dissimilar; varied
9.	i	monarchy:	government led by a king or queen
10.	h	manual:	done by hand

Exercise 2 - Select a Word

1. autobiography
2. paraphrase
3. misappropriate
4. equivalent
5. archbishop
6. manufacture
7. heterogeneous
8. autograph
9. homogeneous
10. symbol

Exercise 3 - Use the Words in Context

1. e
2. g
3. a
4. c
5. j
6. h
7. i
8. b
9. f
10. d

Exercise 4 - Use the Word Correctly

1. I
2. C
3. I
4. C
5. C
6. C
7. I
8. I
9. C
10. C

Exercise 5 - Complete Analogies

1. b
2. e
3. f
4. a
5. c
6. k
7. i
8. l
9. g
10. j

CHAPTER 5

Check your answers for the exercises in Chapter 5.

Exercise 1 - Complete the Word

1. i periscope: a device for seeing around an obstructed view
2. g astronaut: a space explorer
3. j toxins: poisons
4. a animation: creating cartoons
5. c curator: caretaker or manager
6. h bibliophile: book lover
7. b receptacle: container
8. f local: nearby
9. d conductor: leader
10. e refugees: those who flee

Exercise 2 - Select a Word

1. manicure
2. animated
3. toxin
4. captive
5. aquanaut
6. philosophy
7. periscope
8. fugitive
9. conduct
10. locomotive

Exercise 3 - Use the Words in Context

1. f
2. c
3. b
4. h
5. j
6. e
7. a
8. i
9. g
10. d

Exercise 4 - Use the Word Correctly

1. C
2. I
3. I
4. C
5. C
6. C
7. C
8. I
9. I
10. C

Exercise 5 - Complete Analogies

1. e
2. b
3. d
4. a
5. f
6. j
7. k
8. g
9. l
10. i

CHAPTER 6

Check your answers for the exercises in Chapter 6.

Exercise 1 - Complete the Word

1.	g	recede:	to withdraw or move back
2.	d	anthropology:	the study of humankind's development and cultures
3.	f	novice:	beginner
4.	b	fiction:	literature with imaginary characters and a plot
5.	e	preview:	an early look at something
6.	j	megaphone:	a device to make your voice louder
7.	a	hemisphere:	half of the world
8.	c	juvenile:	youth
9.	h	illuminated:	lit up
10.	i	cyclone:	a circular wind storm

Exercise 2 - Select a Word

1. atmosphere
2. rejuvenate
3. anthropologist
4. cyclone
5. factory
6. luminous
7. novelty
8. telephone
9. review
10. concede

Exercise 3 - Use the Words in Context

1. d
2. g
3. b
4. f
5. h or j
6. h or j
7. a
8. c
9. i
10. e

Exercise 4 - Use the Word Correctly

1. I
2. I
3. C
4. C
5. C
6. I
7. C
8. C
9. C
10. I

Exercise 5 - Complete Analogies

1. a
2. d
3. f
4. b
5. e
6. k
7. i
8. l
9. g
10. j

CHAPTER 7

Check your answers for the exercises in Chapter 7.

Exercise 1 - Complete the Word

1.	c	communism:	a social system without private property or classes
2.	f	affectionately:	with tender feelings
3.	e	computerize:	to put information into a computer or transfer tasks to one
4.	j	gratitude:	thankfulness
5.	a	dependable:	reliable; trustworthy
6.	d	hypnotist:	someone who puts another in a sleep-like state
7.	g	illness:	sickness; disease
8.	b	literate:	able to read
9.	h	waiter:	a server in a restaurant
10.	i	interruption:	a break into someone else's speech

Exercise 2 - Select a Word

1. violinist
2. dramatize
3. cheaply
4. quietness
5. respectable
6. reversible
7. multitude
8. happiness
9. conductor
10. interrogator

Exercise 3 - Use the Words in Context

1. e
2. c
3. j
4. g
5. d
6. a
7. f
8. h
9. i
10. b

Exercise 4 - Use the Word Correctly

1. I
2. C
3. C
4. C
5. I
6. I
7. I
8. C
9. C
10. I

Exercise 5 - Complete Analogies

1. e
2. a
3. d
4. b
5. f
6. k
7. g
8. i
9. h
10. l

CHAPTER 8

Check your answers for the exercises in Chapter 8.

Exercise 1 - Select the Word

1. a
2. c
3. b
4. e
5. d
6. a
7. b
8. c

9. benefactor: provider; one who helps others
10. benevolence: good words; acts of charity

Exercise 2 - Select the Word

1. d
2. e
3. b
4. a
5. c
6. e
7. a
8. b

9. inspector: one who examines; an official examiner or checker
10. speculate: look at and consider; wonder about

Exercise 3 - Select the Word

1. c
2. b
3. d
4. e
5. a
6. e
7. b
8. d

9. dictaphone: a machine for recording and reproducing speech
10. predict: foretell; to declare in advance

Exercise 4 - Select the Word

1. a
2. b
3. c
4. e
5. d
6. b
7. a
8. c

9. amortize: to extinguish, as a debt or mortgage; to pay off
10. mortified: to be humiliated; embarrassed

Exercise 5 - Select the Word

1. e
2. b
3. c
4. a
5. d
6. b
7. c
8. a

9. gender: one of two or more categories based on sex or grammatical distinctions
10. genealogy: the study of ancestry or tracing of family trees

CHAPTER 9

Check your answers for the exercises in Chapter 9.

Exercise 1 - Select the Word

1. a   5. d
2. c   6. a
3. b   7. e
4. e   8. c

9. et al.: a Latin abbreviation *et alii* that means "and others." It is used in citing works with several authors. After the first citation lists all of the authors, further references to the same work need only include the name of the first author and the abbreviation et al.
10. alienable: transferable to the ownership of another

Exercise 2 - Select the Word

1. d   5. b
2. e   6. a
3. a   7. b
4. c   8. e

9. conductor: leader or musical director of an orchestra or chorus
10. viaduct: a bridge-like structure, usually supported by arches, that carries a roadway across a valley or other roads

Exercise 3 - Select the Word

1. c   5. e
2. d   6. c
3. b   7. d
4. a   8. b

9. civilize: to bring out of a primitive state; to refine
10. civic: related or belonging to a city or citizens

Exercise 4 - Select the Word

1. c   5. b
2. e   6. a
3. d   7. d
4. a   8. c

9. remit: to send money for payment
10. missionary: a person, usually commissioned by a church, to spread its beliefs

Exercise 5 - Select the Word

1. b   5. e
2. d   6. a
3. c   7. c
4. a   8. e

9. centigrade: a thermometer scale with 100 intervals between the freezing and boiling points
10. centenarian: a person who is at least a hundred years old

CHAPTER 10

Check your answers for the exercises in Chapter 10.

Exercise 1 - Pronunciation

1. no
2. long e
3. 3rd or mo'
4. no
5. no
6. third *o* and *i*
7. cue or queue
8. d and e
9. lock, locale, locate, or loch
10. yes

Exercise 2 - Meanings

1. locution
2. 2
3. lockjaw
4. local
5. places
6. 2
7. lodestar
8. lobe
9. lob
10. locusts

Exercise 3 - Parts of Speech, Derived Forms

1. lobbyist
2. noun or verb
3. lobotomies
4. Lodz
5. locator
6. loco
7. loc. cit.
8. lodgings
9. localized
10. loathsomely

Exercise 4 - Etymology

1. Greek
2. Latin *locus* - place
3. locust; shape, appearance
4. yes
5. Old French word *loge*- shed, small house
6. Scotland
7. guiding star
8. Old English word *lad*- course, way
9. loco
10. *loqui* - to speak

Exercise 5 - General Dictionary Skills

1. earlier
2. look up *loaf*
3. pathology or medicine
4. later page
5. on this page - locus

BIBLIOGRAPHY

Dahl, Hartvig. *Word Frequencies of Spoken American English.* Essex, Conn.: Verbatim, 1979.

Kucera and Francis W. N. *Computational Analysis of Present-Day American English.* Providence, R.I.: Brown University Press, 1967.

Dictionaries consulted in creating this text include the following:

Merriam-Webster, Inc. *The Merriam Webster Dictionary.* Springfield, Mass.: Merriam-Webster, Inc., 1994.

Random House. *Webster's College Dictionary.* New York: Random House, 1991.

Davies, Peter, ed. *The American Heritage Dictionary of the English Language.* Paperback edition. New York: Dell Publishing Co., 1980.

Funk & Wagnalls. *Funk & Wagnalls Standard Dictionary.* New York: Harper-Collins, 1980.